THE
BOXER

Family Favorite

S TEPHANIE A BRAHAM

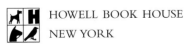 HOWELL BOOK HOUSE

NEW YORK

Howell Book House
Published by Wiley Publishing, Inc., New York, NY

For general information on our other products and services or to obtain technical support please contact our Customer Care Department within the U.S. at 800-762-2974, outside the U.S. at 317-572-3993 or fax 317-572-4002.

Wiley also publishes its books in a variety of electronic formats. Some content that appears in print may not be available in electronic books.

Library of Congress Control Number 00-102745
ISBN 1-58245-127-3

Manufactured in the United States of America
10 9 8 7 6 5 4

Cover and book design by George J. McKeon

Dedication

To my Mother and Father—
who didn't buy me a pony.

Acknowledgments

Many people and organizations contributed greatly to the completion of this book. There were many helping hands!

I would like to thank the American Boxer Club and its members and friends for furnishing valuable information and many of the outstanding photographs in these pages. In addition, I would like to acknowledge the members of the Showboxer and Boxer Mailing Lists (online) for furnishing additional pictures. Special mention must be made of Marcia Adams, whose professional photo concentration on the Boxer for a number of years was so very helpful to me. Appreciation also goes to Pat Mullen for helping to track down some hard-to-find images and to Norman Crook, Rhonda Dyer, Eleanor Linderholm-Wood, Chris Markos, Tom Nutting and Lynda Yon.

When statistical information was needed, friends searched their archives to supply it. Thanks especially to Virginia Zurflieh for never throwing anything away! Heartfelt thanks also to Ted Fickes, who has been our friend and mentor for all these years. Tracy Hendrickson and Michelle McArdle, who work tirelessly in Boxer Rescue, were an inspiration.

I would like to thank my very understanding editor, Nicole Moustaki, who has been a delight to work with from start to finish. Her professionalism has enabled the manuscript to proceed smoothly and without delay.

Finally, I owe a great deal of gratitude to my husband David. His patience throughout this project was greatly appreciated. His artistic eye and the Boxer experiences we have shared for almost thirty years really make up the very fabric of this volume.

—STEPHANIE ABRAHAM

Contents

Introduction

In 1970, my husband and I, newly married, decided to acquire a dog. David thought Gordon Setters were nice, and I wanted a Boxer like Duchess, the dog of my childhood. David informed me that Boxers were pretty ugly, and remembered being disgusted as a child when he saw a friend actually kiss his Boxer full on the muzzle.

Referred by respected breeders, we went to see a litter of Gordon Setters and a litter of Boxers. Both of us, ironically, thought the Gordons were too boisterous for us (that suited me just fine!). The Boxers, mere babes, were of course adorable. We left the breeder's house with no commitments made by anyone—David thought we should think it over, and the breeder wasn't sure we were actually bona fide "show people." I was in tears. Eventually, we returned to the breeder, convinced her that we were good people, and played with the pups some more. That is how the future American and Canadian Ch. Gray Roy's Minstrel Boy ("Casey") came to live with us when he was about 10 weeks old. David was a Boxer convert on the spot.

I remember Casey hanging over the big cardboard box that we had brought with us to carry him home (Crate? What crate?). Such a sweet face! He still had remnants of puppy breath and already displayed a disposition that was gentle and fun at the same time. He grew up a country dog, always with us—even lying at our feet in the local pharmacy/restaurant. The fact that people thought he was striking and beautiful eventually prompted us to take him to a sanctioned match, then some point shows, and the rest, as they say, is history. He finished with five majors and is a Legion of Merit Sire. He never left us until the day he died in our arms.

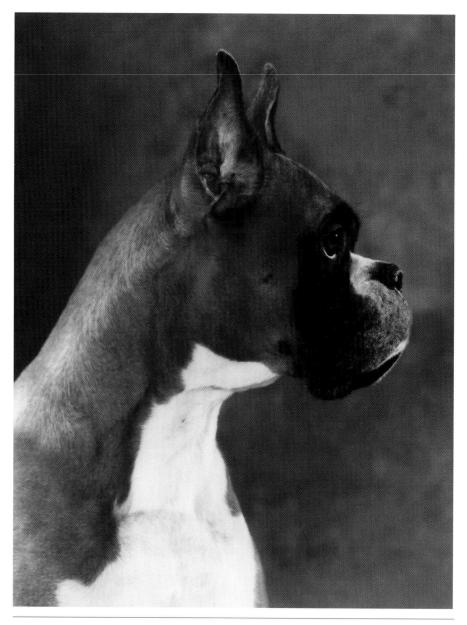

Ch. Gray Roy's Minstrel Boy, LOM "Casey," Legion of Merit sire. (Eduardo)

That is the way Boxers capture our hearts and make their way into the deepest recesses of our psyches. There is something about them—their noble bearing, the way those eyes touch us, their playful nature, their challenge to us to make them obey when they would rather not. That is why people who have once owned a Boxer, who stop you and your dog on the street, always tell you long tales about the special animal they once loved.

The Boxer is exactly what you see. He is a beautiful, regal creature whose clean lines hide nothing. But what most endears him to us is his equanimity with children, his zest for life, his ever wagging tail, the mischief in his soul. Indeed, our lives have been enriched beyond measure because of the love of a dog. We have been adopted by that most irrepressible of clowns, that most intuitive of comforters, that most selfless of companions—the Boxer.

Trefoil's Meistersinger. (S. Abraham)

CHAPTER 1

Meet the Boxer

Congratulations! You have decided to share your life with a Boxer, one of the most engaging of all dog breeds. He will make you laugh; he will make you cry; he will try your patience; he will outwit you when he can. And he will love you with an intensity that will surprise and amaze you. He will be your canine soul mate.

Although the Boxer's origins are ancient (recognizable antecedents appeared in the art of the Assyrians around 1500 B.C.), the breed that we know today was first developed and refined in Germany in the nineteenth century. Used at that time on ducal estates as a hunting dog, the early Boxer was unique in that his undershot jaw was essential, enabling him to hold large and struggling game (wild boar, bear and bison) until the hunter could catch up to the prey. At the same time, he was loyal and loving to his master and protective of his family, especially the children. Though no longer used as a hunter, the Boxer's personality traits of loving and loyal guardianship remain intact.

THE BOXER AT HOME

The Boxer is a bouncy, strong, exuberant dog, always ready for play. He will treasure a favorite toy from puppyhood to old age. It is his distinctive nature to use his front feet to initiate games—suggesting the boxing motion that is commonly associated with his name. He is also quite capable of wagging himself into a shape roughly resembling a pretzel—called *pretzeling,* for the initiated. Not a reliable retriever by nature, the Boxer is still delighted to catch thrown objects and then play keep-away with his owner. Sometimes these escapades can escalate into a game of "Let's not come when called"—not the breed's most endearing trait. If no human is available, the Boxer is quite capable of making up his own amusements and playing all by himself with whatever toy he invents at hand—a sock, a shoe, a paper bag or the family cat. When playtime concludes, he usually is content to curl up in a comfortable spot and wait quietly until something interesting catches his attention. He is generally not a cloying animal and does not demand constant petting and handling.

The Boxer has a natural jumping instinct. Most Boxers are admonished to stay "Down!" all their lives. Some are better at it than others, and their extreme strength makes them a formidable physical presence in the family. Both sexes are totally capable of knocking their owners over—always with the best of intentions. Very small children may be overwhelmed by the ultra-enthusiastic Boxer. If you are lucky, you'll have a sensible dog who will temper his physical size and power to accommodate the little people he adores, for there is no better dog for a child than the Boxer. He gravitates toward children in a room full of adults. He is completely delighted with even the most obstreperous youngster and will tolerate almost all

The Boxer is an enthusiastic dog whose size and strength make him a formidable physical presence in the family. (M. Adams)

manner of abuse with great good humor. I remember a day when I was a child and my mother watched, aghast, as the neighbor's 3-year-old poured sand in our aging Boxer's ears as she lay sleeping. No worry—Duchess simply got up, shook herself and trotted off to avoid the annoyance. The little one lived to tell the tale.

LISTEN TO THE QUIET

The Boxer is known as a "hearing guard dog." One of his great virtues is his relative silence. If you attend a Boxer specialty show, you'll be struck by the lack of doggy noise you hear. That is not meant to imply that your dog has no voice—indeed he does: a deep, booming bark that can approximate a roar in extreme situations when he feels the need to warn. But the Boxer, selective about using his voice, barks sparingly, and then only after thinking the situation over carefully. Usually, he barks only to discourage strange people or dogs from entering his territory. Therefore, he is an extremely effective watchdog. If the stranger turns out to be a friend of the family, the dog will accept the person immediately and accord him or her all requisite rights and privileges. We try not to publicize this fact in the "Burglar Journal!"

INDEPENDENT THINKERS

A Boxer generally needs to know why he should do something. He is not content merely to obey. He learns in a flash, but if you ask him to repeat a trick more than two or three times in a row, he is just as apt to sit down and refuse to perform any more that day. He's bored—as if he's asking, "What's the point?" If you give him a reason (and the best trainers do), he may perform for you with great style. But a Boxer without a reason is a Boxer immovable. This trait is sometimes equated

Boxers tend to be very tolerant of children. (K. Buckley)

with stubbornness, but those of us who know better simply understand that his great intelligence needs to be accommodated before he will act reliably. The Boxer is often a great crowd pleaser: When given his freedom off-lead and instructed to complete a specific routine, he may just take his sweet time about it, visiting with the spectators at ringside and slowly investigating every little piece of ring equipment. Just when the owner or handler is most frustrated—and the gallery is enjoying the dog to the utmost—the Boxer will suddenly complete the exercise without a flaw, never taking his eyes off his owner all the while, and affectionately waiting for the praise that inevitably follows. It's difficult to be angry with a clown.

OTHER BOXER ABILITIES

The Boxer has had great success in the Obedience ring. If the trainer is clever enough to keep the Boxer from being bored, he is a willing and happy worker. Many Boxers do their Obedience routines with exuberant style, often leaping into place at their owner's side in a perfect sit. Boxers have achieved the highest honors at Obedience trials. Likewise, they are natural show-offs in Agility work, loving the challenge of doing complicated physical maneuvers at high speed. Boxers have also achieved Tracking degrees, and many have found their calling as Certified Therapy Dogs. In the past, Boxers were one of the most commonly used breeds as official Guide Dogs for the blind. At present, however, their abilities in this regard have been overshadowed by several other breeds. Many of us would like to see the white or check-marked Boxer reinstated in this role, especially because his highly visible color would be an asset during evening hours.

Boxers are playing an increasingly important role in local law enforcement, working as narcotics detectives as well as guards. They are sometimes used in Search and Rescue missions, and excel at Schutzhund training, an increasingly popular discipline here in the United States.

Boxers are natural show-offs in Obedience and Agility work. (4U2C Photography)

EASY TO GROOM

The Boxer's short coat requires relatively little care. But for anyone who thinks they don't shed, may I tell you that they do indeed. And those short little hairs are the very devil to get out of a sofa cushion or rug. The Boxer actually keeps himself extremely clean, grooming himself almost like a cat. You will continuously see him lick his paws so that they shine. Likewise, he is not a drooler by nature. However, if he drinks water and then shakes his head, the water drops will fly in many directions—onlookers beware! The natural tendency to keep himself clean means that the Boxer is relatively easy to housebreak. If he is crated, he would never dream of soiling his "house." Likewise, he is quick to learn that he must not offend his master's domain.

BOXERS ARE JEALOUS

As a rule, Boxers do not take kindly to sharing their families with any other creatures and are not overly fond of other dogs. Many would be perfectly happy living a long life as the only beloved canine in the household. At the same time, especially as puppies, they love to play with other dogs. And some Boxers seem to enjoy the company of cats, while others will not accept their company at

Jedapay's Jaunty Juba searches for survivors after a California earthquake. (R. Dyer)

The boxer has a short coat that is relatively easy to care for. (LaValley)

all. Almost all Boxers, though, can be taught to tolerate their "own" cats, but if the family feline gets a pat on the head, the Boxer will insist on one, too. And if another dog in the house gets a biscuit treat, the Boxer must have his as well.

Occasionally, this jealous nature can take very serious turns, and the sight of two Boxers fighting is a formidable one. If a family wants to have two dogs as pets, it would be wise to have two Boxers of opposite sexes. They are less likely to come to blows! Years ago, my husband and I owned three male Boxers, all used at stud. They were inseparable for years—ate next to each other, slept in a big happy pile together, romped together. Within two weeks after the eldest dog died of old age, the remaining males—the greatest of buddies—became increasingly irritable with each other. Irritation increased to outright aggressive conflict, and in a few more days these two dogs could never be together again. And that is how they lived out their lives—separately. Clearly, the older dog had established himself as the dominant dog, and the others deferred. When each of the remaining Boxers insisted on Alpha dog status, mayhem ruled. Such is the typical nature of the Boxer.

Boxers can be taught to tolerate a family cat. Here, Jagerhouse's Right Tie and Bog seem to get along just fine. (V. Jaeger)

short muzzle of the Boxer makes him especially susceptible to the torrid heat of a closed car on a warm day. Remember this the next time you run into the grocery store in the summertime and think you'll be back in five minutes. For that matter, no living creature, on any occasion, should be left closed in a car on even a moderately warm day—not even for a minute. Likewise, in the winter, although they love to play games in the snow, Boxers can become chilled if the weather conditions are severe. They are definitely meant to be kept indoors. And they should never be tied out or staked to a tree because they won't tolerate such restraint for any length of time; in their struggles to free themselves, they can easily be injured. I know of one dog who was kept

HEAT, COLD AND WATER

Although Boxers love to play outside, they are not particularly tolerant of extreme heat or cold. On warm days, for example, you must be careful not to run them too hard or they may overheat. The

FAMOUS BOXER FANS

- Humphrey Bogart and Lauren Bacall
- Elvis Presley
- Broderick Crawford
- Rock Hudson
- Shirley Temple Black

- Nat King Cole
- Joan Crawford
- Sylvester Stallone
- Shirley MacLaine
- Jodie Foster
- Ice-T

Boxers like to play games in the snow, but make sure that your dog doesn't become too cold. (V. Jaeger)

Most Boxers have an aversion to getting wet, but Maddie here doesn't seem to mind a bit! (M. Adams)

outside on a "trolley" lead. He repeatedly threw himself against it, and one day he succeeded in breaking his neck. Enough said.

I have found that the majority of Boxers have an aversion to getting wet. Give them a rainy day, and they will want nothing to do with the great outdoors. They are quite capable of looking at their owner with utter disgust at the suggestion that they get their feet wet. At the same time, they are naturally competent swimmers, and some learn to truly enjoy a dip in the family swimming hole or a hunt for frogs at the water's edge. If you have a backyard pool, be sure to teach your Boxer how to climb out safely. And, of course, little puppies and adult Boxers alike should never be near deep water unless supervised by their human families— just as you would watch over a child.

A Lifetime Commitment

Living with a Boxer is an odyssey, full of adventure and fun. Such a journey requires that the human involved take complete responsibility for the welfare of the one creature on earth who will never offer criticism, never complain, and always stand ready to serve and protect. The bond between the Boxer and his family is really no less than a remarkable, caring and totally committed love affair.

BULL BAITING

(From an etching by Joseph Strutt, 1816, courtesy of Norman Crook)

CHAPTER 2

The Boxer Comes of Age

The Boxer as we know the breed today is a product of selective breeding for many generations. However, though his progenitors hark back to heavily built, short-muzzled, courageous dogs in Assyria as early as 2500 B.C., the modern Boxer was largely defined in Germany in the late nineteenth and early twentieth centuries.

After the Franco-Prussian War of 1870–71, Germany entered into a period of relative calm and social stability. A citizenry who had been fighting to survive at last had some leisure and turned to the refinement of a number of already existing dog breeds during the last quarter of the nineteenth century. For example, it was during this period that Karl Dobermann engineered the Doberman Pinscher as a formidable guard, the Great Dane was developed to hunt wild boar, and the Giant Schnauzer emerged from Southern Germany as a cattle dog and protector. The Boxer was developed from stocky "Bullenbeissers" (bull biters), which were used to run down, catch and hold fierce wild game—boar, bear and bison. They were held in great esteem, as written by John P. Wagner in *The Boxer*:

> *Throughout the Middle Ages, the Bullenbeisser was Germany's only hunting hound. . . . they hunt small bears and are taught to tackle them by the ears. This may not work right away due to the tendency of the dogs to bite and hang on so stubbornly that they must be tickled with a long goose quill . . . before they will loose themselves.*

The Bullenbeisser had a wide, short muzzle that distinguished him from all other breeds—then and now. However, after the Napoleonic Wars (1803–15), many of Germany's ducal estates disbanded, and hunting became a less popular pursuit among the gentry. The last recorded boar hunt was held at Kurhesser Courts in 1865, after which the hunting dogs were sold.

During the time that hunting was declining in popularity, the English exported to Germany a particular breed that they called Bulldog but that actually resembled a small Mastiff. This dog was square in proportion and had long legs. Seventy years later, some of the pioneering Boxer breeders in Germany used two of the descendants of these Bulldogs. They appear in the pedigrees of early German Boxers as Trutzel and Tom. Tom sired the white bitch Ch. Blanka v. Angertor (Studbook #4), and she in turn was the dam of Meta von der Passage #30, whelped in 1898, a parti-colored bitch who is the ancestor of almost all Boxers everywhere. Before Blanka, Bullenbeissers were mostly fawn or brindle in color, so it is likely that Blanka and her sire Tom are responsible for introducing white markings to the Boxer as we know him today.

It becomes evident that, in selecting for type and function, the German breeders were developing a smaller and lighter dog from the purest old, heavier Bullenbeisser bloodlines. Though it has been conjectured that the breed resulted from crosses with several other breeds, the Mastiff-like

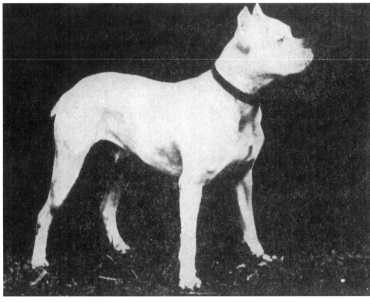

Ch. Blanka v. Angertor, the dam believed responsible for the Boxer's white markings today.

English Bulldog seems likely to be the only significant cross of the century. Any other alliances, such as the Bullenbeisser and the Great Dane, were not perpetuated. As the generations ensued, the Boxer evolved to satisfy some very specific needs of late-nineteenth-century human society.

Bullbaiting was considered great sport in the nineteenth century. It was a terribly cruel pursuit in which the dog was encouraged to attack and hang onto the bull's nose, no matter what the consequences. The bull stood in a shallow depression in the ground, and onlookers cheered wildly from the sidelines. Dogs were kicked, tossed and killed, and the bulls were terrified and exhausted. Of course, wagering attended these dramatic events, and a good bullbaiter was prized by his master and his master's cohorts. There are a number of etchings and lithographs that record these events that were popular throughout England and Germany and elsewhere in Europe. It is not surprising that a dog used to bait bulls would be adopted into the households of cattle dealers and

Friederun Stockmann feeding the Vom Dom Boxers. Sieger Rolf von Volgelsberg (b. 1908) is at the far right. (Stockmann)

butchers, and the Boxer saw duty as a cattle dog as a result of his successes with the bulls. He also gained favor as an excellent circus performer—obedient, intelligent and agile. Unfortunately, his tenacious and courageous nature, as well as his physical structure, encouraged the unscrupulous and cruel to employ the Boxer as a fighting dog—again for the purpose of satisfying the ego of the master, with attendant wagering on the side.

The German pioneers who developed the Boxer were careful and conscientious individuals who recorded their efforts in studbooks and formalized their work by founding the first German Boxer club, called the Deutscher Boxer Club, in Munich in 1896. Other clubs followed, and the first German breed standard was written and adopted in 1902. Bullbaiting was eventually outlawed, and the Boxer was thereafter used as a companion and guard. No one is quite sure where his name arose, but conjecture suggests that it may have something to do with the characteristic gesture with the front feet while playing, which is still

a hallmark of the breed today.

No early Boxer breeders had so great an influence at home and abroad as the famous Vom Dom kennels of Philipp and Friederun Stockmann near Munich. Though not blessed with wealth or material goods, the Stockmanns established a dynasty of Boxers that may arguably be considered the most important ever bred.

THE FAMOUS VOM DOM KENNELS

Friederun Stockmann was born in 1891 and acquired her first Boxer, Pluto, from her future husband when she was an art student in Munich. An extremely talented sculptor, she created wood carvings of Boxers that are highly prized by collectors today. Pluto was registered as the first Vom Dom boxer in 1911. Vom Dom meant literally "from the cathedral," which was the area where Pluto chased cats and basically rendered himself unsociable. Although he eventually had to be placed elsewhere because of his fierce will to fight with other dogs, he had a typical Boxer temperament insofar as people were concerned and was devoted to children. Almost at once, the Stockmanns acquired a bitch named Bilma from the president of the Munich Boxer Club and bred

her to the outstanding Champion Rolf von
Vogelsberg, a brindle dog they had purchased from a
doctor when Rolf was 3 years old. From this litter,
whelped in 1912, came the first Vom Dom champion, Dampf vom Dom. In 1914, Philipp returned
from a show in Hamburg and announced that he
had sold Dampf after he had been awarded the title
of *Sieger* (German for *champion*). At only 18 months
of age, Dampf was exported to America to the
then-governor of New York, Herbert H. Lehman.
Although the first Boxer to be registered in the
United States was recorded in 1904, Dampf became
the first American Boxer champion in 1915.

Philipp Stockmann and ten Boxers that he had
recruited were sent to the front lines during World
War I. The Munich Boxer Club alone contributed
sixty Boxers to the war effort. These dogs, most of
them family pets, were used to guard prisoners, as
sentries, and even to herd cattle. In addition, they
were sometimes sent out to catch and bring down
an enemy soldier—actions that recalled to their
earlier hunting exploits in the forest. Sadly, most of
them did not return home. While those Boxers
were busy on the front lines, Frau Stockmann was
trying to keep her breeding stock alive. Her
resourcefulness was amazing. Times were very
harsh, and just finding food for the dogs was a
great difficulty. As she herself said: "Everything was
sacrificed for our dogs. Even the milk from our
seven goats went mostly for dog food. I bought
what I could on the black market, but it never
seemed enough." (*My Life With Boxers*). There was
not enough food for Germany's human population, and domestic dogs were not valued at that
time unless conscripted into service. At times, the

Philipp Stockmann with two Vom Dom Boxers during World War I.

Vom Dom Boxers were reduced to eating turnips
and offal from the slaughterhouse.

Nonetheless, the Stockmanns and most of the Vom Dom Boxers survived the Great War. Luckily, Rolf returned home—the only one of Philipp's recruits to make it back alive. He was a venerable 11-year-old, but still virile and fit. He won his fifth Sieger title in 1919, with the judge commenting, "Still the beautiful Rolf." He left behind progeny responsible for three of the four foundation sires in the United States, exported by the Stockmanns in order to maintain their breeding program and insure their very lives during the exceedingly tough Depression years of the 1930s. Rolf was also behind the leggy and elegant Zunftig vom Dom, sold to England, who had a lasting influence on the British Boxer.

Between World War I and II, the Stockmanns refined and developed the Vom Dom strain. Always practical, they parted with some of their best both at home and abroad in order to keep the kennels and household intact. Their goals as breeders were many, but prominent among them was the wish to retain Rolf's beautiful head while breeding out his undesirable roached back (a roached back is arched in a way such that it indicates a structural deviation of the correct topline). At the time, admirable head qualities seemed to reside with the brindles, while fawns excelled in body construction. This dichotomy no longer exists in the breed. Through a succession of matings of Rolf's descendants, the Stockmanns succeeded admirably in achieving their goals. Their usual pairing was a beautiful head on one animal with a sound, true body of another until the best dogs could reliably be said to exemplify mostly good characteristics overall.

World War II brought with it more hardships for the Stockmanns. Their son was interred as a prisoner of war, and Philipp was arrested in 1945 and charged with being a war criminal. Although released in September of that year, Philipp's health deteriorated, he was rearrested, and he died in a prison camp hospital in 1946 at the age of 68. Three years later, Frau Stockmann made a memorable trip to the United States, judging a match at which she gave a 13-week-old puppy named Bang Away the Best in Match award (out of ninety competitors). Bang Away remains to this day the top sire and top show dog in the United States, so Frau Stockmann's early opinion of him was a credit to her brilliant eye for a dog. While she was in America, she had an opportunity to see some of the descendants of her great dogs of the 1930s. Luckily, she lived long enough to know that the early promise of those first Vom Dom descendants in the United States would be realized beyond even her wildest imaginings.

Frau Stockmann lived until 1972, breeding her magnificent dogs almost to the end of her long life. Not long before she died, she bred the dog she considered her masterpiece, Godewind vom Dom. He won the Sieger title over 287 Boxers and was declared by the judging panel to be "the most beautiful Boxer in Europe."

THE CORNERSTONES OF THE AMERICAN BOXER

It is generally agreed that the modern Boxer in America owes his existence to four great foundation sires imported from Germany in the 1930s, all of which are described below. Three of them were bred by the Stockmanns, and the fourth was a Vom Dom descendant.

• Sigurd vom Dom of Barmere, a fawn dog whelped in 1929 and imported by Charles Ludwig for Mrs. Miriam Breed of Barmere Kennels in 1934. Notably, Sigurd was the grandfather of the other three foundation sires (the other three Boxers in this list) and sired twenty-six champions. He was 5 years old before his arrival in the United States, and he lived to be 12½. Said Marie Thorne, in *Boxer Club News* in 1945, "To Sigurd more than any other individual dog we owe the tremendous advance in consistent perfect balance of power and elegance." Sigurd was much beloved by his human family, and in those days of benched shows he was always delighted to shake hands with his admirers. Frank Bigler wrote a poem about him upon his retirement from the ring; it was first published in *Dogdom* in 1938:

> *Now his show day's done and the latticed gate*
> *Is forever closed on his battered crate,*
> *And his show-leash hangs on the wall in state*
> *'Mid the trophies of the ring.*
>
> *But Sigurd still roams the sweeping lawn*
> *With none of the beauty or vigor gone—*
> *An athlete modeled in bronze and brawn,*
> *And every inch a king.*

• Dorian von Marienhof of Mazelaine, Legion of Merit, was a golden brindle dog imported in 1935 by John and Mazie Wagner's Mazelaine Kennels. Bred by Frau Tehekla Schneider and whelped in April 1933, Dorian sired forty champions. Jack Wagner considered him his greatest Boxer. Dorian was not defeated in the breed, was a brilliant showman, and never forgot his early Schutzhund training even into his old age. Marie Thorne wrote: "While Dorian was as close to [the] standard . . . as any that ever lived, the first impression he left was rather of great beauty and style." He was the first Boxer to win the Working Group at Westminster (in 1937 over a breed entry of eighty-one) and accounted for twenty-two Best in Shows (BIS). He was the top sire of 1937, 1938 and 1940 and tied with Lustig in 1939.

• Lustig vom Dom of Tulgey Wood, a fawn born in December 1933 and imported in 1937 by Erwin Freund, was the sire of forty-one

Ch. Sigurd v. Dom of Barmere.

Ch. Dorian v. Marienhof of Mazelaine.

Lustig v. Dom of Tulgey Wood.

champions. He was a double Sigurd grandson. Parting with Lustig was one of the most difficult choices that Frau Stockmann ever made, but meager finances and the need to support the remaining dogs caused her to let him go. He came to the United States wearing a collar with the inscription "I am the magnificent Lustig." He took six days to finish his championship in America, achieving a BIS and two Group Firsts en route to his title. During his show career, he won the Group thirteen times and was BIS twice. Lustig lived to be 11½. Marie Thorne wrote, "Lustig was ideal in temperament, never vicious, yet showed great dignity." Frau Stockmann never saw Lustig again, but Philipp did, when he judged at the

Westminster Kennel Club Show in 1938. Eleven years later, Frau Stockmann visited Lustig's grave at the magnificent Tulgey Wood estate. Mazie Wagner eventually purchased the property and designed a Boxer cemetery there. Buried next to Lustig are Dorian, Utz and Ch. Mazelaine's Zazarac Brandy (sire of thirty-four champions). It is a touching memorial to the early years of the breed both in the United States and abroad.

• Utz vom Dom of Mazelaine, Legion of Merit sire, was a fawn dog imported by John and Mazie Wagner in 1939 and whelped in April 1936. Utz and Lustig were full brothers from different litters. Utz sired thirty-seven champions. He won the Working Group at

Dorian vom Marienhof				
	Xerxes vom Dom	Sigurd vom Dom	Iwein vom Dom	Buko von Biederstein
				Zwibel vom Dom
			Belinde von Hassia	Adi von Hassia
				Anita von der Schillerstadt
		Dudel vom Pfarrhaus	Casar von Deutenkofen	Moritz vom Goldrain
				Liesl von Deutenkofen
			Ossi vom Dom	Iwein vom Dom
				Draga vom Schweizer Land
	Andi Saxonia's	Check vom Hunnenstein	Casar von Deutenkofen	Moritz vom Goldrain
				Liesl von Deutenkofen
			Dina vom Hunnenstein	Drill vom Gumpertusbrunnen
				Zitta vom Durrenberg
		Yvonne vom Marienhof	Lauser vom Frankenjura	Egon vom Gumpertusbrunnen
				Adda von Adelegg
			Fee vom Marienhof	Agis vom Schonberg
				Beate vom Marienhof

Westminster, four all-breed BIS and twenty-five Groups before he broke a toe and was retired. He was especially prepotent when bred to Dorian daughters. The legendary judge, Alva Rosenberg, wrote in 1945: "Breed a good Dorian bitch to Utz or Lustig and you seem to hit the jackpot." Utz was the Wagners' cherished house pet until he died of liver cancer on his ninth birthday.

THE KENNELS OF MAZELAINE

From 1934 to 1964, John and Mazie Wagner of Wisconsin bred or owned 123 champions under the banner of their Mazelaine Kennels. Notable among Mazelaine-bred dogs were Ch. Warlord of Mazelaine (BIS at Westminster in 1947, the first Boxer to achieve this distinction) and Ch. Mazelaine's Zazarac Brandy, the winner of an incredible sixty-one BIS as well as BIS at Westminster in 1949. Mazelaine was responsible for the importation of two of the great foundation sires of the breed: Dorian (sire of forty champions) and Utz (sire of thirty-seven champions).

The Wagners were blessed with a rare combination of talents: a real appreciation of breed type and a scientific understanding of the best ways to produce it. The genetic prepotence that their dogs passed on was of singular importance to the breed, and it can be said that most modern Boxers probably trace back to one or more of the animals Mazelaine owned or bred.

Ch. Utz vom Dom of Mazelaine.

Ch. Warlord of Mazelaine.

THE BARMERE KENNELS

It was Mrs. Miriam Breed of Barmere Kennels in New York and later California who commissioned Charles Ludwig to bring Sigurd back to her from Germany. Sigurd went on to sire twenty-six champions in the United States, and the famous Barmere Kennels were responsible for finishing the titles of more than fifty Boxers. In a 1951 interview, Mrs. Breed said, "I shall always be proud that I should have been the one to bring this great dog to America, while he was young enough to accomplish the great good that he did. . . . Even today my little Barmere's Locket is a double Sigurd great-great-granddaughter." Mrs. Breed also imported the sire of the brothers Lustig and Utz, Zorn v. Dom, who gave the breed eleven champions in his own right. She then purchased Dodi v.d. Stoeckersburg in 1933, the first bitch champion in the United States, to be used as her foundation bitch. Dodi's first litter was sired by Check von Hunnenstein. The last Barmere champion finished in 1963. It is interesting to note that Mrs. Breed and the Wagners were actively showing and breeding Boxers during the nearly identical thirty-year span, bearing witness to the infancy of the Boxer in America.

TULGEY WOOD

Mr. Erwin Freund of Illinois finished twenty-seven champions from 1937 to 1947, when he unfortunately passed away. A total of forty Tulgey Wood Boxers finished, partly because of the efforts of the kennel manager, Bob Rogers, who carried on after

Mrs. Miriam Breed with Ch. Barmere's Locket, a double Sigurd great-great-granddaughter, 1951. (Lansdowne)

States—four years after Lustig's death, one of his direct descendants, Ch. Bang Away of Sirrah Crest, was born. He broke all show and breeding records, and changed the breed type forever (see "Headliners" in Chapter 10). After Mr. Freund's premature death in 1947, the kennel was taken over by his manager, Bob Rogers, who died in 1950.

MORE PIONEERS IN THE BREED—UNITED STATES

In addition to the Wagners, Mrs. Breed and Mr. Freund, there was a small but dedicated contingent of Boxer enthusiasts in the United States in the first half of the twentieth century. The American Boxer Club (ABC), the breed's parent club, was founded in 1935. These pioneering enthusiasts included G. J. Jeuther, who finished the second Boxer to attain a championship title in the United States, Ch. Bluecher v. Rosengarten. In 1931, Dr. Benjamin Birk imported German dogs as foundation stock for his Birkbaum kennels; in 1932, Marcia and Joseph Fennessey's import, Check von Hunnenstein, finished as the third U.S. Boxer champion and the first Boxer to win a Best in Show in the United States in 1932; and in 1933, Henry Stoecker of New Jersey finished Dodi v.d. Stoeckersburg, a brindle bitch who was the first to be whelped in the United States (although she was

Mr. Freund's death. Unfortunately, Tulgey Wood ceased with Mr. Rogers' own death in 1950.

Mr Freund's first dog, Tweedle Dee of Tulgey Wood, was bred by the Wagners and sired by Dorian. Mr. Freund's importation of Lustig gave new direction to the breed in the United

Among the celebrity Boxer lovers were Humphrey Bogart and Lauren Bacall, shown here with "Harvey." (Motion Picture and Television photo archive)

Ch. Check von Hunnenstein, first Boxer in the U.S. to win a Best in Show.

German-bred, her dam having come to this country in whelp). She was the first U.S. female champion.

Check von Hunnenstein is especially noteworthy because he was the sire of Dorian's dam, Saxonia's Andl. Check left Germany before he served many bitches, and in the United States he had very little chance to prove his worth as a sire, due to the relatively few numbers of bitches at the time. He was criticized for siring rather small dogs as well as light eyes. Nonetheless, John Wagner speaks very highly of his prepotence and credits him with instilling a lasting elegance and spirit in the Mazelaine line.

In 1934, Mr. Stoecker finished Lord v.d. Stoeckersburg, who was the first American-bred

champion and a half brother to Dodi out of the same dam. In 1936, the AKC moved Boxers from the Non-Sporting Group to the Working Group, where they remain today. This occasioned considerable dismay among many fanciers who felt that the Boxer could not compete against the popular Doberman or Collie. In time, however, their fears were to prove unfounded.

In 1938, Philipp Stockmann of Germany was invited to judge at Westminster Kennel Club. He awarded Best of Breed to the famous Lustig— Dorian could not be shown because his owner, John Wagner, was judging Great Danes that year at the same show. Herr Stockmann attended the ABC annual meeting that week, and his advice was sought in regard to the breed standard. One of his suggestions was that Boxers who were over one-third white be disqualified. Although at least one check had by that time finished his U.S. championship, the ABC adopted the disqualification provision. It remains in effect to this day. It is interesting to note that the motivation for this requirement may stem from the fact that in Germany dogs designated as fit for war duty had to be of a dark color—and the German government rewarded breeders of war dogs with extra food for their families. Easily visible white dogs or parti-colors were less useful, especially at night. As the German standard changed to permit and then eventually disallow these checks, so, too, did the U.S. standard.

In 1940, the first American-bred Boxer ever to win a Best in Show achieved this distinction—Ch. Brace of Briarnole, owned by ABC member Dr. W.

Douglas Schellig. Brace was by Lustig out of Frey of Mazelaine. A short time later, Ch. Serenade of Mazelaine claimed the same honor for an American-bred bitch. American breeders were looking less to Germany and intent on establishing their own type and style. It is interesting to note that during this period in Boxer history in the United States, breeders were not particularly enamored of white markings, and the dogs tended to be much plainer than the favorites today. Serenade, for example, had a black muzzle, barely had white feet and had only a very modest amount of white on her chest.

Even before the Boxer was established in the United States, one member of the breed distinguished himself as a military dog during World War I. Stubby was the mascot of the 102nd Infantry Regiment, 26th Yankee Division. He was gassed, wounded in combat and hit with shrapnel, but he still managed to catch a German spy and save his regiment and one French town. Stubby was decorated for heroism many times, and you can see a touching tribute to him at the First Company Governor's Foot Guard Armory in Hartford, Connecticut. During World War II, many members of the American Boxer Club contributed dogs to the war effort through Dogs for Defense. These individuals included Mrs. Breed, the Wagners, the Palmedos, Mr. and Mrs. Richard Kettles (Warlord's owners) and Mr. Robert Kerns. One especially notable "flying" Boxer was Max, a Boxer paratrooper stationed at Ft. Benning, Georgia, who was presented with his wings after five successful jumps.

Stubby was the first U.S. Boxer war hero.

THE AMERICAN BOXER CLUB

The American Boxer Club (ABC) was founded by a dedicated group of fanciers in 1935. The first ABC National Specialty was held in 1936 as a part of the Greenwich, Connecticut, all-breed dog show, and the first independent American Boxer Club specialty show took place in at the Hotel McAlpin in New York City in 1944. Although the AKC did not require the formation of so-called parent clubs until 1942, the ABC was already an active organization at that time. The early membership rosters of the ABC contain many notable names (among them John and Mazie Wagner, Miriam Breed, Mr. and Mrs. Richard Kettles, Walter Foster, Dr. Dan Gordon and Henry Lark). It is clear that the club was in responsible and dedicated hands from the very beginning. Obedience was promoted at the ABC from 1947–72, then regretfully discontinued due to time and space constraints until 1995. In 1950, there were already twenty-seven member clubs across the nation, and in 1999, ABC membership had grown to 900 individuals and 56 member clubs. (See chapter 13 for further information about the ABC.)

GROWING PAINS

Boxer registrations soared in the 1950s. In 1955 and 1956, Boxers ranked #2 of all breeds. It seemed that almost everywhere you looked, you saw a Boxer. Boxer entries at dog shows often exceeded that of any other breed. Widespread press coverage, the immense popularity of Bang Away that transcended the world of dog shows, as well as the Boxer's natural virtues of a short coat and a tractable temperament contributed to his notoriety. In addition, three Westminster wins at Madison Square Garden—by Ch. Warlord of Mazelaine in 1947, Ch. Mazelaine's Zazarac Brandy in 1949 and Ch. Bang Away of Sirrah Crest in 1951—electrified the general public. Westminster then and now remains a unique event, second only to the Kentucky Derby as the oldest continuously running sporting event in the United States. Westminster winners received so much publicity that the Boxer suddenly found himself "on the map."

While there were many responsible breeders during this era, there were also many who were motivated largely by money—so-called backyard breeders. Health and temperament of the breed

suffered as a result, and the unscrupulous even fought Boxers in pits and used them as fierce guards, trained to attack. Shy Boxers were unfortunately all too common. Happily, the mercurial taste of the public eventually turned to other breeds, and the Boxer regained his stable and happy disposition. The one characteristic that breeders are proudest of, in fact, is the cheerful attitude toward life that has endeared the Boxer to legions of admirers.

INCLINATIONS

The Boxer of the 1960s and 1970s was a very different creature from his progenitors in the 1950s. Breeders sought to build a dog who would still be square but would also be a more elegant, clean-limbed and refined animal, one with distinctly more leg under him than the specimens of prior decades. These height designations have steadily climbed through the years—in the Standard of the 1940s, males were ideal at 22 to 24 inches at the withers, for example, while females were to be 21 to 23 inches. The Standard of today, revised in 1989, recommends that males be 22½ to 25 inches, and females 21 to 23½ inches. If truth be told, animals at the upper ends of these ranges are more admired by the majority of the fancy, and a 22½-inch male today would be considered extraordinarily small in most eyes. Indeed, many top winners exceed the Standard guidelines by a notable margin.

The infatuation with "flash" began after the war years and the arrival of Bang Away on the scene. Sadly, many breeders then and now often select their "keepers" based upon who has the most striking markings, not necessarily the most striking conformation. Hopefully, with the ABC Board of Directors' admonition to judges in 2000 that "plain" Boxers be given equal consideration in the ring, and the increasing numbers of mismarked flashy specimens in the whelping box, breeders will gradually learn to respect and promote the more modestly marked members of the Boxer family.

In 1998, the Boxer ranked #12 in all-breed registrations, and in 1999, he was #10. Cautiously, breeders look to the future, hopeful that the Boxer will not become another guard dog of the moment, with a commensurate surge in popularity. The ABC, ever mindful of these pitfalls, continually admonishes its membership to be responsible in its breeding practices. The Boxer continues to be a formidable presence on the American dog show scene, and competition is keen to attain a championship title, let alone a Best of Breed or Group win. Of all the 147 AKC breeds, the Boxer ranks close to the toughest in the AKC title point requirements—meaning that more Boxers are shown today than most of the breeds made more popular by the general public.

A DOG FOR THE MILLENNIUM

The Boxer is in good hands today, and we trust that he will continue to be responsibly bred, exhibited and loved. From his formative years in Germany, through his refinement in the United States, he enjoys a comfortable existence that could all-too-easily be ruined by a careless disregard for his essential good character and temperament. Luckily, the Boxer's own happy and trusting outlook has so far been justified by his conscientious devotees both here and abroad.

Ch. Hi-Tech Arbitrage, LOM. (Jordan)

CHAPTER 3

Interpreting the Breed Standard

The Boxer breed Standard was adopted by the American Boxer Club membership in 1989 and updated in 1999. It is a blueprint for the breed—a description of the ideal Boxer. A good standard describes the epitome of type—those characteristics that make the breed unique among all dog breeds. For breeders, the Standard is the ultimate guide in their breeding programs; for judges, it provides the basis for their appraisal of the breed in the show ring. Breeder and judge alike, however, recognize that the Standard is a guide and that no individual dog will ever be as perfect as the one the Standard describes. Revisions to the Standard are not undertaken lightly, and the AKC requires that at least five years elapse between such changes. The Boxer breed Standard follows, with interpretations in italics.

OFFICIAL STANDARD FOR THE BOXER

GENERAL APPEARANCE—The *ideal* Boxer is a medium-sized, square-built dog of good substance with short back, strong limbs, and short, tight-fitting coat. His well developed muscles are clean, hard and appear smooth under taut skin. His movements denote energy. The gait is firm, yet elastic, the stride free and ground-covering,

The ideal Boxer should appear "square" at first glance, as does Ch. Sirrocco's Kiss By the Book, shown here. (D. Dennis)

the carriage proud. Developed to serve as guard, working and companion dog, he combines strength and agility with elegance and style. His expression is alert and temperament steadfast and tractable.

This is the perfect Boxer—square, powerful, smooth but muscular, with a ground-covering stride and stable, tractable temperament. Squareness relates to a plumb line dropped from the top of the withers to the ground—this distance should be the same as a line drawn from the point of the forechest to the rear projection of the upper thigh. The dog should appear "square" at first glance.

The chiseled head imparts to the Boxer a unique individual stamp. It must be in correct proportion to the body. The broad, blunt muzzle is the distinctive feature, and great value is placed upon its being of proper form and balance with the skull.

The Boxer's head is unlike that of any other breed. As you will see in the detailed description in the standard, great care is taken

WHAT IS A BREED STANDARD?

A breed Standard—a detailed description of an individual breed—is meant to portray the ideal specimen of that breed. This includes ideal structure, temperament, gait, type—all aspects of the dog. Because the Standard describes an ideal specimen, it isn't based on any particular dog. It is a concept against which judges compare actual dogs and breeders strive to produce dogs. For example, at a Boxer specialty show, the dog that wins is the one that comes closest, in the judge's opinion, to the Boxer Standard. Breed Standards are written, voted on, and approved by the members of the breed parent clubs, the national organizations formed to oversee the well-being of the breed.

to illustrate the perfect head, and breeders must continually strive to produce it. A Boxer who lacks proper head type lacks an essential characteristic of breed type as well.

In judging the Boxer, first consideration is given to general appearance to which attractive color and arresting style contribute. Next is overall balance with special attention devoted to the head, after which the individual body components are examined for their correct construction, and efficiency of gait is evaluated.

Here we are reminded that general appearance—that of the square, balanced dog, with all individual parts contributing to a pleasing whole—is given first consideration when judging the Boxer. Color and style can contribute to this appraisal, but they are not the most important concerns. Special attention must be paid to a correct head. Individual parts of the body are examined in detail, as well as efficiency of movement, but only after the judge has formed an opinion of the overall dog.

SIZE, PROPORTION, SUBSTANCE—*Height*—Adult males 22½ to 25 inches; females 21 to 23½ inches at the withers. Preferably, males should not be under the minimum nor females over the maximum: however, proper balance and quality in the individual should be of primary importance since there is no size disqualification. *Proportion*—The body in profile

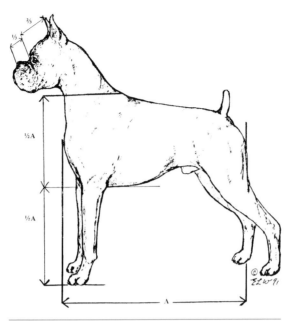

(Drawing from the Illustrated Guide *used with permission of the artist, Eleanor Linderholm-Wood)*

is of square proportion in that a horizontal line from the front of the forechest to the rear projection of the upper thigh should equal the length of a vertical line dropped from the top of the withers to the ground. *Substance*—Sturdy with balanced musculature. Males larger boned than their female counterparts.

The height recommendations tell us two important things— namely, that males can be over the recommended limit, while females should not be. There is a controversy among breeders about this; some feel that there are too many very tall males in the ring and that the use of these animals at stud will promote extreme size in the breed. Common sense should prevail, and we must remember that the Boxer is supposed to be "medium-sized." A taller dog who is to remain square will, of course, have a commensurately longer body to go with his greater height. Correspondingly, judges and breeders should not penalize a male for falling within the recommended guidelines, even if he is smaller than the "fashion" of the times.

Early breeders recognized that the square proportions were essential to allow the Boxer to make quick turns at great speed—an asset during the many maneuvers of hunting game much larger than himself.

Regarding substance, male Boxers should look "masculine" and females should look "feminine." As a rule, the male is taller and has heavier bone and commensurately more muscle development than the female Boxer.

Gender differences are usually apparent in Boxers, the males being bigger than the females. (M. Adams)

HEAD—The beauty of the head depends upon harmonious proportion of muzzle to skull. The blunt muzzle is ⅓ the length of the head from the occiput to the tip of the nose, and ⅔ the width of the skull. The head should be clean, not showing deep wrinkles (wet). Wrinkles typically appear upon the forehead when ears are erect, and folds are always present from the lower edge of the stop, running downward on both sides of the muzzle.

Expression—Intelligent and alert.

Eyes—Dark brown in color, not too small, too protruding or too deep-set. Their mood-mirroring character combined with the wrinkling of the forehead, gives the Boxer head its unique quality of expressiveness.

The eyes of the Boxer are notable in that their mood-mirroring qualities give him "a unique quality of expressiveness." They should be dark brown, affording a gentle expression. Hazel or light brown eyes are not desirable. The eyes should not be round or oblique (slanted), but rather generous and full without being pop-eyed. They must be frontally placed, contributing to the Boxer's soft, almost human expression. Lower eyelids should not be loose. Ideally, the third eyelid should be rimmed with dark pigment.

Ears—Set at the highest points of the sides of the skull are cropped, cut rather long and tapering, raised when alert. *Skull*—The top of the skull is slightly arched, not rounded, flat nor noticeably broad, with the occiput not overly pronounced. The forehead shows a slight indentation between the eyes and forms a distinct stop with the topline of the muzzle. The cheeks should be relatively flat and not bulge (cheekiness), maintaining the clean lines of the skull and should taper into the muzzle in a slight, graceful curve.

The typical and desirable show crop is long and graceful. Natural-eared Boxers (uncropped) may be shown, but the preference of the American Boxer Club, as evidenced in a club vote in 1998, is to continue the tradition of cropped ears. It should be noted that several natural-eared dogs have finished their championships within the late 1990s.

Muzzle—The muzzle, proportionately developed in length, width and depth, has a shape influenced first through the formation of both jawbones, second through the placement of the teeth, and third through the texture of the lips. The top of the muzzle should not slant down (down-faced), nor should it be concave (dish-faced); however, the tip of the nose should lie slightly higher than the root of the muzzle. The nose should be broad and black. The upper jaw is broad where attached to the skull and maintains this breadth except for a very slight tapering to the front. The lips, which complete the formation of the muzzle, should meet evenly in front. The upper lip is thick and padded, filling out the frontal space created by the projection of the lower jaw, and laterally is supported by the canines of the lower jaw. Therefore, these canines must stand far apart and be of good length so that the front surface of the muzzle is broad and squarish and, when viewed from the side, shows moderate layback. The chin should be perceptible from the side as well as from the front.

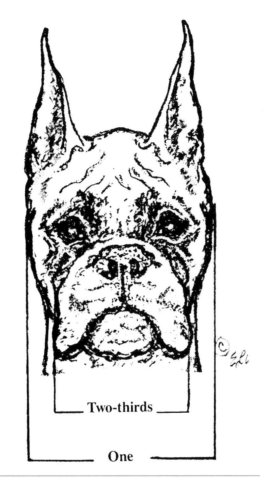

Two-thirds

One

(Drawing from the Illustrated Guide *used with permission of the artist, Eleanor Linderholm-Wood)*

Viewed from the front, the muzzle is ⅔ the width of the skull; from the side it is ⅓ the length of the head from the occiput to the tip of the nose. It is imperative that the tip of the nose lie higher than the stop. This characteristic was instilled in the breed to enable the Boxer to do the work for which he was bred so that he could breathe as he held a mouthful of skin and fur while hunting. This "tip up" is essential to a correct expression as well. The jaw should be broad to accommodate the ideally large, strong teeth. The chin should be visible from both the front and the side, and it must curve slightly upward to accommodate the proper bite. Flews should be generous without being overly pendulous.

As noted above, great value is placed on the proportion of muzzle to skull, and special attention is devoted to the head in its entirety. The head makes the Boxer different from any other breed of dog, and is the essence of type.

Bite—The Boxer bite is undershot; the lower jaw protrudes beyond the upper and curves slightly upward. The incisor teeth of the lower jaw are in a straight line, with the canines preferably up front in the same line to give the jaw the greatest possible width. The upper line of incisors is slightly convex

The head makes the Boxer different from any other breed of dog and is the essence of type; Ch. Trefoil's Strictly Ballroom. (M. Adams)

The Boxer's eyes should be very dark brown and the ears should be long and graceful, as illustrated here in Ch. Cayman's Black Bart. (M. Adams)

with the corner upper incisors fitting snugly back of the lower canine teeth on each side.

Faults—Skull too broad. Cheekiness. Wrinkling too deep (wet) or lacking (dry). Excessive flews. Muzzle too light for skull. Too pointed a bite (snipy), too undershot, teeth or tongue showing when mouth closed. Eyes noticeably lighter than ground color of coat.

The Boxer is undershot—that is, his lower jaw projects beyond his upper jaw. This type of bite gives the dog an almost unshakable grip. However, neither teeth nor tongue should be visible when the mouth is closed. While different heads can comfortably accommodate differing degrees of "undershot," a perfect bite might be illustrated by the lower jaw projecting about the width of a pencil beyond the upper jaw.

The teeth must be of good size and strength for maximum gripping power. Ideally, the canines should be far apart, affording the desirable wide bite. Wry mouths, where the jaws are askew, as well as narrow jaws, seriously

Ch. Berena's Gemini Splashdown, LOM. (M. Adams)

compromise gripping power. Likewise, a curved lower jaw is not desirable.

NECK, TOPLINE, BODY—
Neck—Round, of ample length, muscular and clean without excessive hanging skin (dewlap). The neck has a distinctly marked nape with an elegant arch blending smoothly into the withers.

An elegant, arched neck contributes greatly to the dog's overall appearance. When evaluating height, be aware that a beautiful neck may give the illusion of excessive height where no such fault exists.

Topline—Smooth, firm and slightly sloping.

The topline should be straight but slope slightly from the withers to the tail. The Boxer's back should not lie on a level plane like a tabletop, nor should there be a noticeable dip behind the withers, or any suggestion of a "roach." On the move, the topline should remain firm, with a high-set tail.

Body—The chest is of fair width, and the forechest well defined and visible from the side. The brisket is deep, reaching down to the elbows; the depth of the body at the lowest point of the brisket equals half the height of the dog at the withers. The ribs, extending far to the rear, are well arched but not

The Boxer should have an elegant, arched neck, and the nose should tip up slightly, as demonstrated here by Ch. Rosend's Corporate Raider, SOM. (M. Adams)

barrel shaped. The back is short, straight and muscular and firmly connects the withers to the hindquarters. The loins are short and muscular. The lower stomach line is slightly tucked-up, blending into a graceful curve to the rear. The croup is slightly sloped, flat and broad. Tail is set high, docked and carried upward. Pelvis long and in females especially broad.

Faults—Short heavy neck. Chest too broad, too narrow or hanging between shoulders. Lack of forechest. Hanging stomach. Slab-sided rib cage. Long or narrow loin, weak union with croup. Falling off of croup. Higher in rear than in front.

A natural athlete, the Boxer is designed for speed and endurance, reflecting his origins as a hunter as well as his modern roles of guard and companion dog. While an elegant appearance, especially in the show ring, is attractive and often desirable, he must not be "weedy." Never must there be anything less than an impression of real substance—the natural consequence of strong bone and superbly conditioned muscle. The deep chest and spring of rib allows ample room for the heart and lungs and aids endurance during extreme physical activity. The tuck-up of the lower stomach was historically important in that there was no pendulous abdominal flesh that could easily be torn by fierce prey.

FOREQUARTERS—*Shoulders*—The shoulders are long and sloping, close-lying, and not excessively covered with muscle (loaded). The upper arm is long, approaching a right angle to the shoulder blade. The elbows should not press too closely to the chest wall nor stand off visibly from it. *Forelegs*—The forelegs are long, straight and firmly muscled and when viewed from the front, stand parallel to each other. The pastern is strong and distinct, slightly slanting, but standing almost perpendicular to the ground. The dewclaws may be removed. Feet should be compact, turning neither in nor out, with well arched toes. *Faults*—Loose or loaded shoulders. Tied in or bowed out elbows.

Ideally, the shoulders should be "laid back" at an angle of 90 degrees. Straight shoulders may be the most consistent fault in Boxers today. Well-laid-back shoulders, in balance with rear angulation, foster a smooth, ground-covering gait with ample reach and drive.

HINDQUARTERS—The hindquarters are strongly muscled with angulation in balance with that of the forequarters. The thighs are broad and curved, the breech musculature hard and strongly developed. Upper and lower thigh long. Leg well angulated at the stifle with a clearly defined, well "let down" hock joint. Viewed from behind, the hind legs should be straight with hock joints leaning neither in nor out. From the side, the leg below the hock (metatarsus) should be almost perpendicular to the ground, with a slight slope to the rear permissible. The metatarsus should be short, clean and strong. The Boxer has no rear dewclaws. *Faults*—Steep or over-angulated hindquarters. Light thighs or overdeveloped hams. Over-angulated (sickle) hocks. Hindquarters too far under or too far behind.

The hindquarters of the Boxer must always be strong and well muscled. They allow the dog to exhibit explosive force on the move and must have sufficient angulation to afford maximum propulsion. However, they must not be excessively angulated so as to render turns difficult and sloppy. The Boxer must be able to twist and turn at high speed with relative ease.

COAT—Short, shiny, lying smooth and tight to the body.

Smooth, tight-fitting coats are ideal. Coarse coats are cosmetically unattractive and sometimes result from improper conditioning or parasites.

The short, tight-fitting coat called for in the Boxer Standard is exemplified in this fawn Boxer, Ch. Heldenbrand's Jet Breaker. (M. Adams)

This brindle Boxer, Ch. Vancroft's Primetime, SOM, exhibits the reach and powerful drive called for in the Standard. (M. Adams)

COLOR—The colors are fawn and brindle. Fawn shades vary from light tan to mahogany. The brindle ranges from sparse, but clearly defined black stripes on a fawn background, to such a heavy concentration of black striping that the essential fawn background color barely, although clearly, shows through (which may create the appearance of "reverse brindling"). White markings should be of such distribution as to enhance the dog's appearance, but may not exceed one-third of the entire coat. They are not desirable on the flanks or on the back of the torso proper. On the face, white may replace part of the otherwise essential black mask and may extend in an upward path between the eyes, but it must not be excessive, so as to detract from true Boxer expression. *Faults*—Unattractive or misplaced white markings. *Disqualifications*—Boxers that are any color other than fawn or brindle. Boxers with a total of white markings exceeding one-third of the entire coat.

While there may be individual preferences for fawns or brindles, both colors are equally acceptable. Likewise, reverse brindles are no more or no less acceptable than the "red" brindles—those dogs with relatively few stripes. In general, breeders prefer the shades of fawn tending toward red, rather than pale or "washed out" coloration.

White markings are often attractive but must not exceed ⅓ of the ground color (disqualification). There is no requirement that the Boxer have white markings. The preference of many breeders and judges is for the "flashy" look that appealing white markings convey, but overall quality of the dog is much more important than whether or not he has a white collar, high white stockings or any other white markings. Indeed, too much white on the face often has a deleterious effect on proper Boxer expression. Likewise, white up the thighs, over the hocks or in other inappropriate locations is unattractive and distracting.

It is not unusual to have totally white or almost totally white Boxers born in a litter. Members of the American Boxer Club are currently pledged not to breed or register these dogs. While they are therefore ineligible to compete in the Conformation show ring, these dogs can be exhibited successfully at Obedience, Tracking and Agility trials. There is a small percentage of white Boxers who are deaf. These animals can be trained successfully to hand signals if the owner is patient and willing.

GAIT—Viewed from the side, proper front and rear angulation is manifested in a smoothly efficient, level-backed, ground covering stride with powerful drive emanating from a freely operating rear. Although the front legs do not contribute impelling power, adequate "reach" should be evident to prevent interference, overlap or "sidewinding" (crabbing). Viewed from the front, the shoulders should remain trim and the elbows not flare out. The legs are parallel until gaiting narrows the track in proportion to increasing speed, then the legs come in under the body but should never cross. The line from the shoulder down through the leg should remain straight although not necessarily perpendicular to the ground. Viewed from the rear, a Boxer's rump should not roll. The hind feet should "dig in" and track relatively true with the front. Again, as speed increases, the normally broad rear track will become narrower. *Faults*—Stilted or inefficient gait. Lack of smoothness.

The balance of front and rear angulation of the bones enables the Boxer to cover ground with an effortless stride, while maintaining a firm topline. He must have adequate reach to prevent interference of the front legs with the driving rear. This essential structure of front and rear is designed to give the Boxer maximum power to chase and maneuver. If there is an imbalance of front and rear angulation, the efficiency of the gait will be greatly compromised, and the dog will be forced to make some accommodation to avoid striking his front and rear legs on the move. This may manifest itself in "straddle stepping"—moving very wide behind—or in a crabbed, shortened stride.

CHARACTER AND TEMPERAMENT—These are of paramount importance in the Boxer. Instinctively a "hearing" guard dog, his bearing is alert, dignified and self-assured. In the show ring, his behavior should exhibit constrained animation. With family and friends, his temperament is fundamentally playful, yet patient and stoical with children. Deliberate and wary with strangers, he will exhibit curiosity but, most importantly, fearless courage if threatened. However, he responds promptly to friendly overtures honestly rendered. His intelligence, loyal affection and tractability to discipline make him a highly desirable companion *Faults*—Lack of dignity and alertness. Shyness.

The character and temperament of the Boxer make him unique among dogs. He should be fearless, ready to defend and protect. However, he should also readily accept strangers who are welcomed into his household. Shyness or misplaced aggression should

The Boxer's intelligence, loyal affection and tractability to discipline make him a highly desirable companion. At attention here, Ch. Huffland's Obladah of Arriba. (M. Adams)

never be tolerated—or perpetuated in a breeding animal. Such faults of character are most often genetic in nature—sometimes a difficult thing for a breeder to admit. As John Wagner said in his 1945 lecture entitled "Judging Fundamentals":

Last, but not least, we have temperament. Temperament is governed by the nervous system and no dog wholly can display his type and quality unless he has that spark that makes him alert and active. A dog with real temperament will outwork a dog of equal physical qualities on sheer nerve alone. The judgment of temperament should never be overlooked, though it often is. It is the electric system that makes a machine work and if it is feeble you have a pretty sluggish job.

CONCLUSION OF STANDARD—The foregoing description is that of the ideal Boxer. Any deviation from the above described dog must be penalized to the extent of the deviation.

This sentence was added and ratified by the ABC membership in 1998, and approved by the AKC in February 1999. Its intent was to give judges and breeders a yardstick by which to measure the severity of faults. In other words, dogs should be faulted only to the degree to which they deviate from the ideal; for example, slightly loaded shoulders should be faulted less than severely loaded shoulders. This may seem simplistic to some, but the clarification has been helpful to many.

DISQUALIFICATIONS—Boxers that are any color other than fawn or brindle. Boxers with a total of white markings exceeding one-third of the entire coat.

Approved February 5, 1999

Effective March 31, 1999

Some Boxers are alleged to be solid black. If so, this is a disqualification. However, the majority of so-called black Boxers are instead reverse brindles, with such heavy striping that the fawn base coat is barely visible. Reverse brindles are perfectly acceptable.

It is sometimes problematic to determine if a particular dog is more than ⅓ white—after all, we have no precise measure. However, animals with full white collars, white stockings to the elbows, white up the thighs, white up the rib cage and generous white on the face are undoubtedly over the limit—especially if one notes that these same animals, if theoretically pinned on their backs, have full white stomachs beneath. Practically speaking, many judges are loath to disqualify an animal who may be "borderline" in their judgment. Breeders, however, should beware of excess white and take care not to promote flash to the exclusion of quality.

The Standard is a description of perfection—a dog that none of us will ever see. And it is also open to a certain degree of interpretation—my idea of a "slightly sloping" topline may be different than your idea of the same characteristic. But many elements of the Standard are unequivocal—the proportion of muzzle to skull, the insistence on excellent temperament by any reasonable measure, the precise definition of squareness, and so on. If all breeders and judges studied and understood the Standard in all of its simplicity and at the same time all of its complex detail, perfection might be closer at hand.

(M. Adams)

CHAPTER 4

Finding the Right Boxer for You

Before you actually begin to search for your perfect Boxer, you should read and learn as much about the breed as possible. If you have friends who own Boxers, it would be a good idea to interact with their dogs if you can. You may decide that a Boxer is not the dog with which you want to share your life. They are not for everyone. If you are looking for a quiet animal who won't be underfoot and will basically keep to himself unless called, the Boxer will not please you. A Boxer wants to be near you at almost all times. He is active, joyous and not always instantly obedient to commands. At the same time, he is devoted, loyal, loving and trustworthy. Please do not make the mistake of purchasing a Boxer only to discover that your personalities do not mesh. Do your homework!

WHAT TO LOOK FOR IN A BREEDER

Most reputable breeders have spent years developing bloodlines that produce dogs with sound minds and bodies. Such breeders have a wealth of knowledge about conformation, health and temperament issues—all of which may affect your personal enjoyment of the dog who is to be your beloved pet. The horrific commercial kennels that breed solely for profit and the "backyard breeder" who produces a litter from a less-than-sound bitch bred to the neighbor's dog are not the best places to purchase your puppy. Although those circumstances just might produce the occasional perfectly acceptable Boxer, the odds are certainly better if you find a serious breeder, someone who will perhaps be willing to be your mentor for life. Such a person is an invaluable asset to both you and your dog; nothing can take the

If you buy your Boxer puppy from a breeder, make sure that the kennel is reputable and that the bloodlines of your puppy are sound. (M. Oki)

place of the years of experience that a caring, intelligent breeder has gained while striving to breed that elusive perfect Boxer.

FINDING A BREEDER

There are many ways to find the right breeder for you. One of the best sources is to contact your local kennel club and ask for a list of reputable breeders in your area. If you do not know the local kennel club, contact the AKC for appropriate sources (see Appendix A, "Resources," for the details). The AKC also can provide you with the name, address, and phone number of the contact person for the American Boxer Club, the national parent club for the Boxer in the United States (appendix A). The ABC representative can provide you with Boxer breeder information for your locale, as well as contact information for the local Boxer club in or near your area, a great resource and a place to meet fellow Boxer enthusiasts and breeders.

Ads in the newspapers, while they may indeed be placed by reputable breeders, do not come with any recommendations or referrals—invaluable information when you are searching for a loving companion. Purchasing a Boxer from a pet store is not advisable. Beware of the adorable puppy in the cage—he may well be ill or a product of indiscriminate breeding from commercial kennels. Although we have all at one time or another been tempted to "rescue" such a cute puppy, there are considerable risks involved in doing so. The so-called guarantees of a pet store may not be enforceable.

As you expand your search, you may come across breeders who are a long distance from you—perhaps thousands of miles—or perhaps a faraway breeder is the only one with the bloodlines you decide are essential. Although it is possible to purchase a puppy based on photographs and pedigrees provided by a breeder, I recommend that you actually see the Boxer who is going to go home with you. Photographs can be deceiving, and temperament is hard to evaluate over the phone. The breeder may be honest and totally forthcoming with information and disclosures, but only you can determine which dog is your best personal choice.

After you decide where to buy your puppy, you must decide whether to buy a male or a female. (M. Adams)

joy and a challenge to live with.

Males are, of course, physically larger than their female counterparts, but the female Boxer is also quite capable, in a burst of enthusiasm, of accidentally toppling Great Aunt Mabel or Tommy the Toddler. So don't look to the female to be sedate and always gentle.

I personally find the males to be less independent than the females—even more "connected" to me and wanting to be with me at all times. If you don't want such constant attention, perhaps a female Boxer is best for you.

Keep in mind that, if not neutered, a male Boxer is going to be attracted to any female dog in season, no matter what the breed. All the training in the world may not render him obedient if he wants to play Romeo.

Whether to purchase a male or a female dog is a very personal choice, but both make wonderful family companions. You may not decide until you actually look at a litter of puppies or an older dog and one of them "speaks" to you with his or her eyes.

MALE OR FEMALE?

Ask ten Boxer owners whether they prefer a male or a female, and you will probably receive a split verdict. Although there certainly are differences associated with gender, all typical Boxers are gifted with the ebullient temperament that makes them a

AKC REGISTRATION

The American Kennel Club is the registering body for the vast majority of purebred dogs in the United States. Such a registration is *not* a guarantee of conformation, health or temperament, but it is an invaluable record. The registration certificate contains the name of the breeder, the registered name of your dog (usually but not always supplied by the breeder), the registered names of the sire and dam of your dog and the dates that they first appeared in the official AKC Studbooks that trace the breeding record of those animals used for procreation. Every registration also contains a unique number with which an individual dog can always be identified.

In addition to your dog's vital statistics, the registration indicates whether your dog is to be used for breeding or whether he is instead sold on a *limited registration*. Dogs with limited registration may not be bred, but they enjoy all other privileges afforded to them by the AKC.

If you should ever decide to sell or give away your Boxer, you can officially transfer his ownership by filling out the transfer portion on the back of the registration and sending it to the AKC.

Not all purebred Boxers are registered, however. Occasionally, a purebred Boxer may not be registered. This often happens to white Boxers who are not intended for breeding. If the Boxer you choose has not

Whether or not your Boxer is AKC registered, he will still make a dutiful and loving companion. (McCarty)

been registered, he can still participate in AKC performance events (Obedience, Tracking, Agility), but you must first apply for and obtain an Indefinite Listing Privilege (ILP) number from the AKC. ILP dogs must be spayed or neutered. Contact the AKC registration department for details.

PERMANENT IDENTIFICATION

The AKC requires very careful record keeping of its breeders. Increasingly, it also is advising breeders and owners to implant microchips to permanently identify individual dogs. This tiny computer chip—the size of a grain of rice—is inserted just under the skin on the back of the dog's neck. The code number stored in it can be read by a handheld electronic scanning device. This number can then be checked against a master list containing contact information for the owner of the dog. If your dog is recovered after being lost or stolen and is subsequently scanned for a microchip, you may be on your way to recovering your dog.

The AKC Home Again Companion Animal Recovery program records all microchip numbers, regardless of chip manufacturer, to aid in tracing and identification should it become necessary. As of this writing, 20,040 lost pets had been reunited with their families worldwide through this program.

If your Boxer was not microchipped by the breeder, you can have a chip inserted later. Most animal shelters and veterinarians are equipped to do so, and it takes only a minute. Contact the AKC to register your own animals with Home Again.

Tattoos are another means of permanent identification, although they are being largely supplanted

by microchips these days. Usually a designated number, the tattoo can be placed in the groin area or inside the ear flap. For the time being, the AKC's Home Again program registers these tattooed numbers along with microchip numbers, so a recovered dog can be reunited with his owner should they become separated.

DNA testing is becoming more and more popular in the breeding community. Each individual dog can be DNA tested via a simple blood test or saliva swab, whereby the dog's genetic blueprint is revealed. DNA testing insures that pedigree records are accurate and aids the AKC in reviewing the breeding practices of specific kennels. If there is ever a doubt about the parentage of an individual dog and DNA records are available, appropriate scientific judgments may be made.

THE INITIAL INQUIRY

When you contact a breeder for the first time, you should ask a number of questions. It's a good idea to make a list of the things you want to know so you won't forget something important. Be prepared to answer many questions yourself—a good breeder will want to get to know you and your family. You probably will be asked whether or not you have owned a Boxer before, have a fenced yard and intend to show or breed—in short, the breeder will be developing a profile of you.

The more questions the breeder asks you, the more you will know that she really cares about her dogs. Do not be insulted if the breeder is not entirely happy with your answers to some of her questions. Try to be objective and look at the

Pick of the litter? There are four American champions and four Canadian champions in this bunch! L–R: Am./Can. Ch. Syrr Run's Line of Credit; Syrr Run Lineup Lolita; Am./Can. Ch. Syrr Run Line of Vision; Am. Ch. Syrr Run Line of Design; Can. Ch. Syrr Run's Line Drive; Am./Can. Ch. Syrr Run Line Dancer v. Rion. (Horne)

TESTING A PUPPY'S TEMPERAMENT

Formal step-by-step processes have been devised for evaluating the temperament of 7- to 9-week-old puppies, and I've provided here the ones that I think are most appropriate. Take care to perform them using common sense and a gentle hand.

- **Reaction to Strange Objects:** Place a non-threatening object in a room with each puppy individually. This could be something like a book, log or pail—almost anything to which the pups are not accustomed. You should note whether or not the puppy investigates and, if he does, whether he ignores or interacts with the object, either of which is acceptable. Fear that is not immediately overcome may be a sign of shyness.

  You can also perform a second test with objects that make a strange noise, such as rattling pebbles in a jar or dropping something like a saucepan. Take care not to overdo the noise—you don't want to hurt the puppy's eardrums! Clearly, the pups who react with curiosity, even if they startle initially, can be predicted to grow up with more stable dispositions than their littermates who run for cover.

- **Dominance Test:** Quietly place the puppy on his back and gently but firmly hold him in place. Do not let him squirm out from under your hand to right himself, which is his natural instinct. When the puppy calms down, let him go and watch his reactions. Does he take off to the far corner of the room and cower? Or does he react positively and come right to you, tail wiggling? The latter reaction is obviously to be preferred. Beware of the puppy who refuses to calm down under your hand. Such a pup may grow up to have more aggressive tendencies than you would like to see. On the other hand, the passive puppy who immediately accepts your dominance without any struggle may grow up to be shy or lack sociability.

- **Recall Test:** Take the puppy away from his littermates and place him in a nonthreatening environment. Quietly walk away from him and sit down on the ground to face the pup. Call him to you with a happy and enthusiastic tone of voice. The best reactions are for the puppy to either run right to you with abandon or come more reservedly but still exhibit happiness to be with you. Beware of the pup who totally refuses to come or actually runs away.

- **Follow Test:** Take the puppy away from his littermates and place him in a nonthreatening environment. While walking away from him, call the pup to follow you with a happy and enthusiastic tone of voice. The best reaction is for the puppy to run willingly after you, tail wagging, happy to be near you. This is the pup who exhibits typical Boxer temperament. As with the Recall Test, beware of the pup who will not follow, hides, or runs away.

Clearly not all testing is foolproof. Be careful not to frighten a puppy who may be perfectly stable. And above all, ask the breeder's permission before performing any tests.

WHAT ABOUT AN ADULT DOG?

There are many reasons why a breeder may offer you an older puppy or adult Boxer. She may have kept a promising puppy to show who didn't quite turn out the way she had hoped. Or the breeder may have taken back a dog of her breeding who was being mistreated or who had bad luck due to family circumstances of illness or divorce. Such a dog may be ideal for you—he may be totally housetrained, so you won't have the bother of seeing to this yourself. His ears may be standing, saving you the trouble of many taping sessions. He may have been trained to respond to commands, making him a responsible canine citizen and less boisterous than a puppy. For example, this could be beneficial if you are caring for an elderly adult human who is infirm. Do not ignore the adult Boxer—he could be your best choice, depending on your own personal circumstances. Remember, a puppy is only a puppy for a very short time, and it is the adult dog who will live with you for many fulfilling years.

Puppies are great, but you might find a faithful companion in an adoptable adult Boxer. (M. Adams)

RESCUE ORGANIZATIONS

There are many organizations around the United States and throughout the world that are organized to rescue and foster Boxers who have been victims of bad luck or bad placement. You can find out about these organizations through the American Boxer Club or the AKC (see Appendix A). The majority of rescue workers are tireless in their devotion to the breed and are among the world's most selfless people. They give their time, their energy and their total emotional commitment to dogs who ask for so little but demand much.

Rescued dogs may be in need of veterinary care and immediate housing. For instance, they may need to be signed out of a pound in a hurry before an impending euthanasia. In addition to whatever urgent action may be required, the dog's temperament will be assessed. This enables his rescuers to place him in the best-possible permanent

Michele McArdle, head of Rescue in Connecticut, has placed over six thousand Boxers in the last seventeen years (including this one). (McArdle)

environment—with or without other dogs, cats, small children and so on.

For all the rescued Boxers waiting in foster homes and shelters, you can do a very good deed by adopting that one special dog who needs you to love. If you wish to breed or show, remember that you will need accompanying registration papers.

PET OR SHOW QUALITY?

First, let me say that most of us who show Boxers were drawn to the breed in the first place because of the lovely temperament of these sweet and energetic dogs. In my own household, all the show dogs are also pets who sleep on the couch or play with their doggy toys in front of me while I'm watching TV. So there is absolutely no conflict between the pet and the show environment, unless the dog is actually at the show venue itself. However, the conformation of the pet may not quite equal that of the show-quality animal. You may be uncertain whether or not you wish to breed or show your Boxer, which is perfectly understandable. In this case, the breeder can explain to you all the costs and commitments related to the show and breeding world. It is no small matter to finish the AKC championship of a Boxer in the United States. It often involves the employment of a professional handler and definitely requires a substantial amount of money. On the other hand, if you are especially dedicated and are a talented owner-handler yourself, you can dispense with the professional assistance and keep at least some of your money in the bank.

Breeding your dog is also a potentially expensive proposition. Not every whelping is a joyous experience ending with a litter of healthy pups. There are sometimes sad stories relating to birth complications and death of mother or babes. In addition, breeders spend many, many hours—some of them the wee hours of the morning—to make sure that even the healthiest of pups grows up to his full potential. Do not be surprised if your breeder suggests that you consider purchasing a bitch with breeding potential, whether or not she is a bona fide show prospect. Sometimes the only difference between a puppy whom the breeder keeps to show or breed is a matter of markings and color—sheer window dressing—with little or nothing to do with actual breed-Standard quality. I'll discuss this more fully in Chapter 9, "Beauty and Brains: Obedience Trials, Performance Events and Other Fun Things." If you are able to purchase a very representative, temperamentally sound and especially well-bred bitch for future breeding, you will have made the first step toward what might be an exciting future with Boxers.

CONTRACTS

Some breeders will ask you to sign a contract with them when you purchase a puppy. The contract may be fairly simple. For instance, it may specify only a few things, such as the purchase price, a commitment to neuter the pup at an appropriate age if he is not being sold for breeding, as well as a guarantee that the puppy will be kept in a fenced yard and not allowed to run loose in the neighborhood.

If the puppy is to be shown or bred, the contract probably will be more detailed. For example, it may specify your responsibility to achieve an AKC championship with your Boxer. The sale may also involve co-ownership of the Boxer. For a bitch, the co-ownership may include an agreement to breed her to a mutually agreeable stud dog with one or more puppies going back to the original breeder. For a dog (male), the co-ownership may require a portion of future stud fees over a certain period of time to be paid to the breeder.

There are as many contracts as there are people to write them. Many are enforceable in a

Showing your Boxer can be challenging and fun. Ch. Heldenbrand's Jet Breaker, winner of the ABC Best of Breed in 1990, is shown here winning at the ABC Regional in 1989. (Booth photo)

court of law, so be careful what you sign. For the most part, contracts are made so that all parties have a record of the understanding they had on the day the puppy or adult went home to new owners. Time has a way of blurring good intentions, so it is an excellent practice to have all agreements in writing.

WHAT TO EXPECT WHEN YOU PICK UP YOUR PUPPY

When you arrive at the breeder's home or kennel to actually take your puppy home, you and the breeder both have responsibilities to each other and to the puppy.

Your Responsibilities

Before you make the trip to pick up your puppy, there are a few questions you need to ask the breeder so that you go to the kennel prepared.

First, ask what form of payment he or she will accept. Some breeders accept cash, a money order or a cashier's check, but not a personal check. You definitely don't want to be sent home empty-handed on such a special day. While you are undoubtedly an honest person, the breeder may have been stung by the unscrupulous in the past.

Second, ask what type of food the puppy has been eating. You should purchase the same food and have it waiting for your puppy when he comes home. Even if you eventually decide to change the food, don't run the risk of upsetting the pup's digestion by making a radical food change right away. Some buyers even bring empty plastic jugs with them to the breeder's home so they can be filled with the water to which the puppy is accustomed.

Third, pack the following items in your car: a collar, a leash, a crate, a blanket, and lots of paper towels. Be sure that your puppy is wearing the collar and leash when you leave the kennel—even if your puppy is not yet accustomed to a collar and leash, they offer a measure of security so he can be controlled in the unlikely event that any emergency interrupts the car ride home. Of course the crate will help with that as well. And the blanket and paper towels will come in handy in case of accidents or car sickness—after all, your puppy may never have ridden in an automobile before this day.

> ### PUPPY ESSENTIALS
> Your new Boxer puppy will need:
> food bowl
> water bowl
> collar
> leash
> ID tag
> bed
> crate
> toys
> grooming supplies

In addition to meeting your puppy's physical needs, your easiest task, and the most important one, is to provide lots of love and patience after you get home. You have done your breeder homework. You have chosen the right Boxer for you and your family. Now it is time to enjoy the dog who will return your affection beyond measure for the rest of his life.

The Breeder's Responsibilities

The breeder should provide you not only with your chosen puppy, but also with two documents: your Boxer's pedigree and a transfer of ownership—either an AKC Individual Dog Registration Application (IDRA) form or the actual permanent registration certificate from the AKC.

If the breeder registered the litter but not the individual Boxer you are purchasing, she will provide you with an IDRA form. The IDRA is what the AKC sent to the breeder when she first registered the litter, and she will have one form for each puppy in the litter. Either you or the breeder will complete the information on the back of the form to transfer the ownership of the dog to you and to specify the name under which the puppy should be registered. This registered name will be the name by which your Boxer is forever known to the AKC; it can never be changed or expunged, so it should be chosen carefully (see the accompanying sidebar). The breeder often reserves the right to choose a dog's registered name; the breeder is the one who has spent the time, effort and money to produce this puppy, it should be her privilege to name him if she desires.

To actually register your Boxer, you must submit the IDRA to the AKC with the requisite registration fee. The AKC will subsequently send you the official permanent registration certificate for your Boxer.

The breeder should also provide a copy of the puppy's pedigree. Usually, at least three generations

NAME THAT DOG

Every dog registered with the AKC has a *registered* name, his official AKC-recognized name, and a *call* name, the everyday name to which the puppy answers.

The registered name usually contains the "kennel name" of the breeder—a designation of her choosing that may be well recognized in the Boxer world. For example, the name of the kennel owned by John and Mazie Wagner is Mazelaine Kennels. They incorporated their kennel name in this registered name: Mazelaine's Zazarac Brandy. They could have just as easily named him Zazarac Brandy of Mazelaine.

If the breeder does not care what you name the puppy, you can invent your own kennel name for your Boxer's registered name. The AKC requires the name to be twenty-five or fewer characters, but that's the only limitation. Beware not to register your puppy with anything inappropriate to his adult status. He won't be "Itsy Bitsy's Cutestuff" for long!

The name you want your dog to recognize when you want his attention—that is, when you "call" him—is entirely up to you. The AKC doesn't keep track of call names. The call name is often a derivative of the registered name, but it doesn't have to be. For example, the call names for two Mazelaine dogs were Dorian and Brandy, both derived from their registered names, but they could just as easily have been Rover and Dandy. The call name can be anything that you as the owner want it to be—whether or not the breeder has already chosen one. Just be careful not to confuse a puppy who thought he already knew his name!

should be listed. If the breeder fails to do this or gives you fewer than three generations, you can request, for a fee, a more complete genealogy from the AKC. (If you received an IDRA rather than a permanent registration, you can make your request on the back of that form.) While the names of your puppy's predecessors may not seem important to you at the time of purchase, they may become very important if you decide to breed or show.

There are a lot of details to consider on the day you bring your Boxer puppy home. (S. Abraham)

Likewise, if you are purchasing an adult, the breeder should supply you with all the same documentation. However, rescue animals are likely to come into shelters or rescue organizations without any documentation whatsoever. Do not be surprised if there is no pedigree available. If you are a very lucky "rescuer," and the former owner has surrendered them, registration papers will gladly be supplied.

(M. Oki)

CHAPTER 5

Living with Your Boxer

Boxers are easy to love. They can also be frustrating and even baffling to the uninitiated. The Boxer demands respect and attention—he is not a windup toy. He thinks. He invents games. He knows your moods and responds in kind. He weaves himself into the fabric of your household with a velvet paw. Like children, Boxers need rules and gentle discipline. He must not be ignored and relegated to a basement or an empty room—he needs to be an integral part of the family for the span of his life.

WHY A CRATE?

A dog crate is a safe haven that may save your pet's life one day. It is not a prison; it is not cruel. Every Boxer should be trained to walk quietly into his crate when his owner wishes it. From the first day that your wiggly puppy enters your home, a crate should be waiting. You will find that the crate is a godsend. It is a great aid in housebreaking. A Boxer will be loath to soil his crate—it is not in his nature. If you leave a puppy to roam around the kitchen or the laundry room while you are absent, you are quite likely to come upon a "mistake" waiting for you in some far corner of the room. But a crate will usually remain dry and clean. When you return, immediately let the puppy outside to do his business. He will oblige right away, and it doesn't take very many days before your Boxer associates his needs with the out-of-doors. If he continually leaves unwanted presents while loose in a room, he may never get the idea of what housebreaking is all about.

There are many different crates available on the market, and you can purchase them from kennel supply houses and pet stores. Some crates are made entirely of strong wire; some are heavy plastic. All are easy to clean—an important consideration. Wire crates often fold up like a suitcase for ease of transport. Plastic crates usually break down into two halves, have a wire mesh door and are quite sturdy; they're excellent choices if your dog needs to take a plane trip. They are a bit less drafty than the wire crate on a cold day but are also warmer on a hot summer day. Heavy aluminum or wooden crates are also available—usually at considerably higher cost than the plastic or wire crates. They are excellent choices if they are within your budget, though a wooden crate may be subject to a dog's chewing problems, and wood or metal is often heavier to carry than wire or plastic.

Whichever crate you use, be sure that any wire mesh is not so large that a puppy can poke his head through—this is very important because the pup may not be able to retract his head, causing him panic and considerable stress. This will not be a consideration after the first few weeks—puppies grow exceptionally fast! Be sure to place a cushion or a towel or some other bedding on the bottom of the crate so your Boxer will be comfortable.

Just as you would fasten your child into an appropriate car seat designed for his safety, it is wise for your dog to travel in a crate if the size of your vehicle permits. In the unexpected motor accident, the crate acts like a seatbelt to keep your dog from being ejected from the car; it will also keep him from running loose on the highway and possibly being struck by a passing car. In your home, the crate keeps a puppy—and an adult—from many dangers. He will not be able to eat a potentially poisonous house plant, chew on electrical cords or outlets or eat your grandmother's handmade quilt. Although he may dislike the confinement at first—be prepared for whimpering and soulful pleas for freedom—you will be amazed one day to see your Boxer actually enter his crate of his own accord, curl up and go to sleep. It offers him a respite

A crate is an essential piece of equipment, especially when traveling. (S. Abraham)

from noisy children, reruns on TV and bickering adults. He will actually grow to *like* it. So will you!

A puppy can be crate trained from the time you bring him into your home. I recommend feeding the puppy in his crate so that he associates it at once with pleasant experiences. You may choose to leave the crate door open, but place the food dish inside. If you need to do errands outside the home, do not crate the puppy more than a few hours at a stretch during daylight hours. After all, he deserves your time and attention; the crate should not be used as an all-too-convenient baby-sitter. You may find it practical to crate your puppy at night when the household is asleep, but be prepared for protests at first! It is wise to leave a soft blanket and a safe toy with the pup at night so he doesn't feel so alone. You might even keep the crate in your bedroom so the pup can be reassured by your presence.

FENCES AND RUNS

A fenced yard or a fenced-in area is a must for your Boxer. He must never be allowed to run loose in the neighborhood. Many dangers lurk about for unsupervised dogs—automobiles, poisons, aggressive animals, fearful neighbors. Remember, to the uninitiated the Boxer is merely a version of a Pit Bull, and hysteria may reign. I heard of an elderly Boxer in New Jersey who unfortunately escaped from his yard. He was quite

It is important for your Boxer's safety that he be kept confined. Here, two dogs enjoy their exercise pens at a dog show. (S. Abraham)

deaf and almost blind. When a neighbor called the police to protect her from what was surely a rampaging Pit Bull, the officers obligingly shot and killed the Boxer. Country dogs are no less at risk. In my own rural town, a farmer shot an adolescent Boxer because he was chasing the farmer's geese.

There are many different types of fences. Any of them are appropriate, so long as your dog cannot escape either by jumping, digging or climbing. Chain-link fencing is an excellent choice. A height of 4 feet might keep the average Boxer inside solely because it will never occur to him to jump over the barrier. But to those who delight in escaping, even 6 feet will prove a mere annoyance. Your Boxer can easily sail 6 feet in the air from a standstill. We once had a Boxer who used the chain-links as toeholds and thought climbing was great recreation. So watch and be wary! Solid-wood fences are also quite appropriate and offer the added advantage of preventing your dog from looking at an attractive nuisance (like the neighbor's Poodle) on the next property. So-called invisible fences might work well, but you won't know until you try, and installation is an expense to be reckoned with. The invisible fence requires your Boxer to wear a collar outfitted with a device that will give him a startling, though harmless, shock if he walks over the boundaries you have established (more on collars on p. 63). Beware that some dogs are not impeded by this device, whereas for others it works perfectly for a lifetime. Whether or not it is effective for your Boxer, remember that it will *not* prevent the neighbor's dog or the stray raccoon from strolling over to pay a visit.

A dog run is a smaller area, usually made of chain-link fencing or heavy wire mesh. Runs are sold as portable units of varying dimensions: 4 × 12, 6 × 20 and so on. While they don't allow for much exercise, they do meet the need to keep your dog secure and safe. In addition, if your Boxer is an escape artist, the run can be covered to keep your pet in bounds. The floor of the run

Boxers are capable of jumping over fairly tall fences. Be sure that yours is high enough to keep your dog on the correct side. (A. Keil)

can be grass, gravel, asphalt or concrete. It should be cleaned daily. If you are leaving your dog in the run while you are away, be sure he has a shelter—a lean-to or a doghouse—so that he can escape inclement weather or excessive heat or cold. At boarding kennels and other professional facilities, runs are often attached to indoor kennel enclosures. At home, you may be able to attach the run to your garage, a shed or even a room in the house itself.

An exercise pen is a small portable unit made of wire link. It is sold in various heights and can be folded up for easy transport. It is invaluable when you are traveling, visiting nondoggy friends who don't have fencing, or raising small puppies who need their outdoor exercise. We use pens that are 4 feet high. You must never leave your Boxers unattended in exercise pens because they can be easily tipped over. Wire covers are available that fit across the top of the pen and discourage jumpers, climbers and "tippers."

Regardless of what fencing you choose, you'll quickly be glad you installed it. If you can arrange it so that the dog is within fenced bounds when you let him out, it will save you a great amount of time spent walking your Boxer on a leash—especially to be appreciated in monsoon rains or freezing weather. Remember that you do not need a huge fenced area; your Boxer will survive quite happily in a modest yard.

PUPPY-PROOFING

Every household contains objects that are potentially harmful to a curious puppy. Remember to treat him as if he has the intelligence and energy of a toddler, and you will do all the right things! See to it that electrical cords and outlets are not accessible. Take care to lock away cleaning solutions or other potentially poisonous substances (including antifreeze). Be sure that toxic plants are out of reach: Many common plants, as well as garden and wild specimens such as water hyacinth, many fungi, castor beans, nightshade and monkshood, may prove deadly to your dog if ingested. If you are treating your lawn or garden with chemicals, keep the puppy away so that he cannot walk on the grass, lick his paws and ingest the dangerous and even fatal toxins. And dogs do not tolerate chocolate, so keep the candy bars secured. Watch for poisonous snakes and toads in some areas of the country. Supply your puppy with safe toys to satisfy his urge to chew, and you will save the furniture as well. If you own a swimming pool, be sure that your puppy does not have access to it unless you are watching; even though a puppy may instinctively swim, he tires easily and may have no idea how to exit the pool. Adult dogs likewise should be carefully supervised around water.

HOUSETRAINING

Housebreaking your Boxer will be easy, but it does require you to make an effort to train your puppy properly. One of the most important aspects of housetraining is patience, and the other is a proper schedule—a repetitive, reliable routine of feeding, as well as a schedule of sleep and play. It makes sense not to feed your puppy late at night or allow huge gulps of water just before bedtime. As your puppy becomes accustomed to his own needs to go outside, and knows when he will be able to meet them, he will become more trustworthy in the house.

The Boxer is a naturally clean breed. You will often see your Boxer licking himself, much like a cat, to keep spotless. Infant puppies who can barely stand will toddle off to the corners of their box to eliminate, thereby saving their living quarters from fecal dirt. A puppy in a crate will never want to soil the quarters in which he is sleeping, and this is one of the reasons why a crate is so important in your puppy's life.

When you return home after leaving your puppy in his crate for a half-hour or more, *immediately* take the puppy outside to do his business. Do not wait to unpack the groceries or answer the telephone because the excitement of your arrival may cause the pup to make a mistake. If the puppy sleeps in his crate at night, it is imperative that you be there to take him outside at the first sign of wakefulness. Praise him lavishly when he eliminates outside. Once the pup has the right idea, he will be naturally reinforced every time you repeat

Be sure to puppy-proof your home, as Boxer pups can find plenty of ways to accidentally harm themselves and can be quite naughty! (M. Adams)

the routine. It is wise to use one particular corner of the yard for training, and you will find that the puppy will go back to it time and again—making cleanup a lot easier for you.

Since the pup will not and should not be crated constantly, it is important that you take him outside just about every time you think about it—definitely after every meal and whenever he wakes up from a nap. My husband housebroke our first Boxer before the pup reached 12 weeks of age, but they were outside about every hour and several times at night. If you are willing to put this sort of heroic effort into your goal of a perfectly housetrained dog, you will reap great rewards. I do not advocate paper training at all because it will merely tell your puppy to use newspapers and won't teach him that the ideal goal is to evacuate in the yard. Never rub the pup's nose in any mistakes that he makes, either, because this teaches him nothing at all except to wonder at the strange behavior of humans.

TOYS

To a Boxer, life is a continual game. Toys are an essential part of that game and thus must be safe and sturdy. Hard nylon bones and natural knuckle bones are both virtually indestructible and unlikely to splinter

The fun-loving Boxer will be undaunted by toys the size of his head. (S. Abraham)

and are excellent choices when your dog feels the urge to chew. Though Boxers are not notorious chewers, almost any dog enjoys a good session with a bone now and then.

Vinyl toys, often sold with squeakers inside, are great fun, too, but watch to make sure that your dog does not dismantle and eat them, squeaker and all. Likewise, it is not a good idea to offer knotted socks or nylon stockings, because a Boxer is quite capable of swallowing these items, which can be dangerous and require surgical removal if they become lodged in his intestines. Also, he cannot be expected to distinguish between toy socks and good socks, so it's better not to tempt him in the first place.

Balls are a great source of fun. Your Boxer may toss the ball around by himself or play a brilliant game of "catch me if you can," daring you to take the ball from him. Tennis balls are too small for Boxers; be sure you use a large, soft ball that cannot be swallowed in one great gulp. One of the most popular toys at my house is a huge vinyl soccer ball that can be squished between the dog's jaws. When it's dropped, it reinflates, making the most delicious whistling noise as the air reenters—it amazes and delights every time.

Having the right kinds of toys for your Boxer can provide him with a great deal of exercise. (Tomita)

Soft fleecy toys are also greatly coveted. The dogs never tire of carrying them about. I always think the toys must feel pleasant in the dogs' tender mouths.

Do not give your Boxer rawhide products, so-called chew hooves or pig's ears. They can spell disaster for your dog, and we never offer them because they can easily become impacted in their intestines.

Like human children, Boxer pups will turn any interesting object into a toy. (E. DeGroff)

Maxine, a brindle Boxer, looks skeptical. (S. Lehmann)

A soft Frisbee may be easier for Boxers to catch because of their undershot bite. (Tomita)

No matter which toys your Boxer enjoys, there are several incontrovertible truisms associated with them.

- Two dogs will always want the same toy, no matter how many are arrayed before them.

- Almost anything may become a toy if your Boxer desires it.

Boxers can make a game out of toilet paper rolls, playing cards, any accessible part of a houseplant, your children's dolls or your spouse's slippers. Nothing is sacred. And don't be surprised if your dog enjoys playing all alone. This activity is part of the breed's delightful nature, and Boxers invent the most intricate toss-and-catch games to amuse themselves.

COLLARS AND LEADS

Our Boxers wear collars only when they are being walked on a leash or trotted around a show ring. At home with us, inside or outside in their fenced yard, a collar is not a part of the wardrobe. Collars can be dangerous in many situations although necessary in others. For example, an active dog like a Boxer can snag his collar on just about anything—a tree branch, a crate door or the jaws of a playmate. We know of an instance when one dog, playing happily with another, caught his jaws in his friend's collar. The two dogs twisted and panicked, and even though the frantic owner was present, trying desperately to free the struggling dogs, one of them suffocated before her eyes.

Boxer pups find fun in everything—even a plain old paper towel—which is why it's very important to watch them carefully so they don't find anything potentially dangerous to play with.
(L & B Horne)

Collars are mostly a convenience for us, an easy way to pull a dog in one direction or another, and are useful during training. But ask yourself if a collar is really necessary for your dog to wear all of the time. Identification tags are obviously useful when attached to a collar if your dog becomes lost, but why would this happen? If you are in a situation where such identification is advisable, then use the collar. In most instances, though, and surely with a dog who is safely fenced, a collar does not need to be worn very often. Of course, it is advisable to equip your Boxer with permanent identification in the form of a microchip or tattoo in case he does become lost (see chapter 3).

There are several different types of collars. Choke collars offer the most control because they can be alternately tightened on your dog's neck. They come in both nylon and chain varieties. Be sure the nylon is strong enough for a rambunctious Boxer, and remember that even the sturdiest chain collars can suddenly break at their weakest link. Prong collars, capable of inflicting actual pain on your dog if he resists them, are not necessary and would be considered cruel by most Boxer lovers. Flat collars, which must be carefully sized so that your dog cannot escape them, come in a variety of materials, usually nylon or leather. Remember that they, too, can cause your dog harm if they become caught on something dangerous. Any collar must be chosen with regard to the strength of the loop that attaches it to the leash. If that loop is weak, the collar may come apart. For recreation or the show ring, we have found that nylon collars work best for us.

Leashes, or leads, are usually made of leather, nylon or metal chain. A show lead, usually nylon, is customarily short, only 3 feet long. You may find it convenient when walking your dog to have either a 4- or 6-foot-long lead. There are also retractable leads on the market that afford your dog 16 or more feet of length—suitable for jogging him on a playground, or a hiking trail. Such retractable leads are rated for strength based on the weight of the mature dog. I recommend the strongest variety made, because a 75-pound adult male Boxer sometimes seems to have the strength of Samson! Remember to evaluate the sturdiness of the catch mechanism that attaches the lead to the collar. It must be sufficiently sturdy to keep your dog in check and well-constructed so that it can't fall open or break easily. Do not forget that the collar and lead apparatus are only as strong as their weakest component.

Boxers should never be tied up to a tree, a doghouse, a fence, or anything else. For one thing, they will absolutely hate the confinement, and they will not grow resigned to it. Their struggles may actually injure them; remember that they can easily jump over a fence or a railing and strangle on the lead. In addition, a dog who is tied cannot effectively defend himself and may actually become aggressive out of fear. Likewise, many Boxers do not tolerate the pulley type of runs—a wire strung between two posts (a clothesline, for example) with the dog's lead attached to the wire so that the Boxer can trot up and down along it. An adolescent puppy we sold to very well-meaning people broke his neck as he continually flipped himself in the air, trying to escape such a device.

Consider carefully when it is advisable for your Boxer to wear a collar. Here, Brentwood's Blue Knight wears a light nylon variety. (R. Zurflieh)

Horror stories notwithstanding, your Boxer will certainly spend much enjoyable time with you when he is being exercised on a collar and leash. He will look forward to such recreation and will become excited when he sees the leash and collar in your hand. A well-trained dog, neither pulling nor lagging behind his owner, is a satisfying sight. Just be careful to always take your dog's safety into account.

BASIC TRAINING

Boxers are extremely intelligent and a challenge to train. They are not robots, doing the bidding of their owners unceasingly. A Boxer wants to know *why* he should do something, even though he learned *how* to do it in only a few minutes. I still remember my father laughing as my childhood Boxer, Duchess, stoically refused to jump over a low fence that my dad had built in the backyard. She had done what he asked once, twice and three times. But upon the fourth request, she simply sat down, wagged her tail and became immovable. Such is the Boxer.

"Come"

The most important command your Boxer will ever learn is "Come." He should perform willingly and reliably, as you may one day be urging him away from danger when you want him by your side. Many Boxers instinctively respond to their owner when they hear the emphatically spoken command "Come" and the owner at the same time claps his hands happily and motions the dog to him. A food treat, given when the dog obeys, is an excellent idea at the beginning of training. Your dog will associate the command with the treat, and learning to Come will be a pleasant experience.

If your dog does not respond to the Come command when he is loose, you may wish to put him on a collar and lead. Walk away from him to the end of the lead, then ask him to Come. If he does not, gently but firmly tug him to you, praising lavishly when he approaches, and give him a treat when he arrives. Repetition will certainly teach the dog what you want, but the real test will come when the dog is off the lead and you have no physical control over him. Now your Boxer will have to *want* to obey, so be sure that you have made the exercise fun and happy. If you are too stern, your dog may look at you with a twinkle in his eye and run in the opposite direction. Be sure to exercise considerable self-control if this happens because the last thing you want to do is scold your dog when you eventually catch up to him. He'll *never* come if you really lose your patience.

If you have a persistent problem in getting your Boxer to respond properly to Come, ask yourself if he receives too little exercise. Sometimes a dog who is closely confined can't resist tearing around once free, seemingly oblivious to his master's wishes. Ironically, giving the dog more freedom may solve your dilemma.

"No"

Just the sound of the command "No," sternly spoken, is enough to deter most Boxers from whatever it was they were doing at the time. Repetition, if the situation occurs again, will definitely teach the dog that the behavior he was exhibiting is unacceptable. Housetraining is probably the discipline that most often occasions the use of No. Jumping runs a close second. It does not take a canine genius to learn that No means business, and a dog as sensitive to your moods as a Boxer will understand immediately that he had better pay attention.

"Down"

"Down" is the most difficult command for your Boxer to obey. For centuries, the Boxer was bred to pursue and hold large game until the hunter could approach. To that end, the Boxer had to be able to run and jump up at the prey animal (boar, bear or bison). Jumping as a form of greeting is as natural to a Boxer as walking, and he may persistently leap upon newly arrived visitors if he is excited or really, really happy. Although you may enjoy his exuberant displays, remember that he is quite capable of knocking an adult man to his knees. Small children and the infirm may not appreciate a Boxer's enthusiasm. So, you and your Boxer have your work cut out for you.

I must say that I honestly have never learned how to reliably keep a Boxer's four feet on the ground. No matter how many thousand Nos a

However innocent and adorable, even the youngest puppy needs some discipline. (S. Abraham)

Boxer has heard in these situations, he will still test your correction. A sweeping downward motion with your hand and arm, accompanied by the firm verbal command, will be understood almost at once by most Boxers and may deter him—for a moment. I have tried (gently) stepping on his hind toes when he jumps; he will get down, of course, but he may not be discouraged the next time he wants to launch himself in the air. Age is the only thing that calms him in this regard, and I have simply learned to watch and be wary when my Boxer is excited. If you have a Boxer who doesn't jump, consider yourself fortunate. However, those of us who love the breed have learned to take jumping in stride and simply deal with it as best we can. One saving grace of the breed is that the initial "jump greeting" will eventually be followed by quiet and more decorous behavior; you may simply have to wait about ten minutes before the calm reigns.

OBEDIENCE SCHOOL

A good obedience training school is an excellent choice for developing your Boxer's good manners. Trainers are often veteran "dog people" who instinctively understand how to motivate an individual dog to perform at his master's will. Such a school will not only teach your dog some useful lessons in obeying, but will

Obedient Boxers get to have fun! (M. Krecji)

also help him to become socialized among strange dogs. Training class should develop your dog's self-confidence and strengthen the bond between him and his master.

Heeling may be one of the most difficult lessons for your Boxer to learn. His natural exuberance will not be conducive to the restraint of a lead and matching his bold stride to yours. Hopefully, the trainer will recognize the breed's special antipathy to this command and will be able to work effectively to modify your Boxer's behavior. Many a Boxer does brilliantly in Obedience work and thoroughly enjoys the more advanced lessons relating to jumping over a fence, selecting certain scent articles and retrieving.

The Down command is a difficult and important command to teach your Boxer. (K. Nevius)

ESTABLISHING DOMINANCE

Remember always that the Boxer is an astonishingly intelligent creature. Therefore, you must teach him immediately that you are his pack leader, the one who must be obeyed. Wolves establish a pecking order in their packs, where all pack members acknowledge their place in the hierarchy. So, too, must your Boxer be taught to obey the people in his household pack. His primary caregiver should be the one who makes sure that any attempts by your dog to evade his responsibility to obey are met with gentle but firm resistance. I am not advocating punishment as a form of teaching, but I do recommend that you repeat whatever exercise your Boxer chose to ignore or avoid. Let him know you are well aware that he was not compliant, and encourage him to obey the next time.

You will find that your Boxer responds with great joy to human interaction and attention. You are a god in your dog's life, and he will happily worship you as such. He will be acutely sensitive to your moods, whether joyous or sad; he will pine when he is left alone; he will be most content when he is by your side—anywhere and everywhere—even including your sojourns to the powder room or the mailbox. Do not forget that he deserves the same devotion from you that he so willingly gives in return.

(M. Adams)

CHAPTER 6

Keeping Your Boxer Healthy

With conscientious care and a little good luck, you should be able to enjoy your Boxer's company for ten years or more. Though not as long-lived as some breeds, recent advances in breed-specific medical research will hopefully enable your dog to live on into a comfortable old age. Your Boxer's best ally in the quest to keep him healthy is you, his owner, the person who spends the most time with him and the one who can recognize a problem at its very first manifestation. Trust your instincts, and if you have any questions or concerns, consult your veterinarian immediately.

Most Boxers are very good patients when they are ill. They willingly stand for examination and wag their tails through minor medical procedures in a veterinarian's office. Ask for local anesthesia whenever possible—in the Boxer, this will suffice for the removal of small skin tumors and the suturing of minor wounds. Boxers have a relatively high threshold for pain and discomfort, although they probably will let you know immediately when they're not feeling up to par. They will plead with their eyes and cling to you when they are not feeling well.

SELECTING A VETERINARIAN

The best veterinarians are good listeners. They pay attention when you speak to them, because they realize that you know your dog best. Be wary of the veterinarian who can never take the time to consult with you, is constantly interrupted in his examination, belittles your medical observations, or doesn't seem to like your dog. Your choice of a good veterinarian is critical to your Boxer's good health. The best medical professionals are keenly interested in your insights and observations. Their offices do not have to be elaborate, but they should be clean. Likewise, the staff members should be courteous and helpful, because they will be your Boxer's caretakers in the event that an overnight stay is required.

If your Boxer's breeder lives in your area, ask him or her for a recommendation. You can also contact breeders of other types of dogs in your area. Breeders undoubtedly will have very strong opinions borne of long experience. Consider contacting people in dog-related professions, too—local groomers, handlers or obedience instructors. Call the all-breed kennel club in your area if there is no Boxer club nearby. You need to know who you can trust at a time of crisis, who knows the medical idiosyncrasies of the breed and who is likely to be available in case of a crisis. You don't want the "second string" if your dog's life depends on the expert.

If at any time you have serious questions regarding the competence of a particular vet, remember that most states have veterinary licensing boards. These boards oversee the practicing veterinary professional, and are an excellent sounding board and information source.

When you have precious pups like these, you want to be able to find a veterinarian that you like and trust. (M. Adams)

PREVENTIVE HEALTH CARE

Your Boxer's first line of defense against illness is you, the one who sees him daily. You must be alert to any signs that indicate a deviation from his usual state of good health. You may notice subtle changes before anyone else does, even your veterinarian. Perhaps your Boxer seems slightly less enthusiastic about his morning walk, drinks more water than usual or has decided not to eat. Trust your observations: Follow up on your suspicions with a closer look, and seek professional help if your dog continues to exhibit worrisome symptoms.

Vaccinations

When you purchased your puppy or adult Boxer, he undoubtedly already had one or more

Your Boxer's first line of defense against illness is you. Here, four generations of healthy Boxers relax on the grass: Ch. Somerset's Lady Liberty (age 10), Brentwood Astin Martin (age 6), Ch. Somerset's Alfa Romeo (age 7½) and Ch. Brentwood's Lexus (age 4½). (R. Zurflieh)

YOUR PUPPY'S VACCINES

Vaccines prevent your dog from getting infectious diseases such as canine distemper and rabies. Vaccines are the ultimate preventive medicine: They're given before your dog ever gets the disease so as to protect him from contracting it. That's why it is necessary for you to have your Boxer vaccinated routinely. Puppy vaccines start at 6–8 weeks of age for the five-in-one DHLPP vaccine, and then every three to four weeks until the puppy is 18 weeks old. Your veterinarian will set up the proper schedule for your puppy's vaccination regimen and will remind you when to bring in your dog for shots.

vaccinations administered while under the breeder's care. Adult dogs need to receive booster shots approximately once a year, but puppy vaccinations are more frequent. These shots are administered to prevent certain communicable diseases and are manufactured in either killed- or modified-live-virus form. They stimulate your Boxer to produce antibodies to the specific disease for which they are formulated.

When our pups reach 6 to 7 weeks of age, we give them a so-called puppy shot. This consists of a combination of distemper, hepatitis, parainfluenza (so-called kennel cough) and parvovirus vaccines. Timing is everything. A young puppy may still have antibodies against disease that were passed to him by his mother during the first twenty-four

hours after birth through the first milk, known as colostrum. At a variable rate, these natural antibodies disappear over time. Until they are gone, the shots that we administer will not have the proper effect. Therefore, to be safe, we give shots every two to three weeks until the puppy reaches 18 weeks of age, when even the most long-lasting maternal antibodies will have vanished. At 12 weeks, we add leptospirosis protection into the combination we are using and continue with that regimen through the 18-week-old mark. In our New England area, many vets are discontinuing leptospirosis vaccines because they believe that the occasional and sometimes serious reactions to the shot are not worth the small risk of contracting the disease. However, it is spread via contact with infected urine, often that of rodents. Because our dogs live in the country where they inevitably come in contact with mice and squirrels and might be vulnerable to this potentially fatal malady, we continue to vaccinate against it.

When pups reach 6–7 weeks of age, we give them their first puppy shot—usually a combination of vaccines for distemper, hepatitis, kennel cough and parvovirus. (S. Bell)

Many breeders ask their veterinarians to give bordatella and corona virus vaccinations. Bordatella protects against certain strains of kennel cough (of which there are many), and Corona protects against the gastrointestinal virus of the same name.

We choose not to vaccinate for these diseases because we believe that the parainfluenza component of the booster is adequate for cough protection against the most common upper-respiratory viruses and that corona is neither common nor deadly in our area. Your veterinarian should advise you of the circumstances in your area.

Rabies is a threat in many areas of the United States and is an invariably fatal disease. Rabies vaccinations are given to puppies at about 4 months of age, sometimes earlier if there is severe danger in that region. We do not advocate giving the combination booster and rabies shot all at once, as this may be too much of an assault on your dog's immune system. However, many veterinarians continue the practice. Consult your veterinarian for his or her recommendations. Standard protocol advises a second rabies shot at 1 year of age, followed by a booster every two to three years.

INTERNAL PARASITES

A variety of internal parasites can infect your Boxer, both as a puppy and as an adult. Fortunately, most infections can be prevented or easily eliminated. All de-worming medications are potentially toxic, so do not buy over-the-counter preparations. Always rely on your veterinarian for advice. Most parasites can be detected by routine fecal examinations. Nemex (pyrantel pamoate) is a very safe drug that is excellent for removal of roundworms and hookworms, and it can be used safely even on very young puppies. It requires no fasting.

Roundworms (*Ascarids*): This is a common parasite, especially in puppies. Signs of infection include a dull coat, failure to thrive and a potbellied appearance. Your dog may come down with mucus-like diarrhea and pneumonia due to migrating larvae in the lungs. Roundworm eggs are ingested when your Boxer eats infected soil and feces, and it can be transmitted to people. Despite a breeder's best efforts, many pups are born with a roundworm infection acquired from the mother before they were born.

Be sure to keep your Boxer free of parasites; here, Ch. Arriba Talisman Epitome is the picture of health. (M. Adams)

It is not uncommon to see roundworms in your dog's stool. They are stringy and white and may be elongated or coiled. In severe infestations, a puppy may vomit worms. Because an adult female roundworm can lay up to 200,000 eggs daily, early detection and elimination are imperative. In rare instances, roundworms can be fatal to a puppy.

Hookworms (*Ancylostoma*): These thin, translucent worms live in the small intestine and exert their influence on the host by attaching to the intestinal wall and sucking blood. As they move to new feeding sites, the old wounds they have caused ulcerate and continue to bleed. Thus, a puppy heavily infested with hookworms may develop a profound, fatal anemia. Pale gums; dark, tarry stools; diarrhea; weakness and emaciation are all clinical signs of hookworms. Adult dogs may harbor a chronic infection with less dramatic

symptoms. In the most serious cases, blood transfusions may be necessary.

Whipworms (*Trichuris vulpis*): These are sometimes difficult to detect in fecal exams because whipworms shed their eggs intermittently. Repeated testing may be necessary. Adult whipworms live in the cecum, a pouch in the large intestine. Signs in a light infestation are minimal, but severe infections produce weight loss, poor coat and diarrhea often streaked with fresh blood. Whipworm eggs do not survive in dry areas, and regular cleaning of any moist spots in the yard or kennel run will help to control infections.

Tapeworms (*Cestodes*): These parasites are transmitted to the dog via an intermediate host, the flea. Tapeworms can be up to 70 centimeters long, and segments resembling grains of rice are passed in the feces. You may even see these segments move in freshly passed stools. Tapeworms cause general colic, mild diarrhea and occasionally a lack of appetite. Effective flea control is needed to interrupt the life cycle of the worm.

Heartworm (*Dirofilaria immitis*): This is a serious disease that is often fatal without treatment. The worm itself is transmitted in larval form by the bite of an infected mosquito. Microfilariae circulate in the bloodstream and develop into adult worms. These worms live in the heart muscle itself and cause symptoms related to circulatory disturbances. These include weakness, coughing, intolerance to exercise, respiratory distress, weight loss and sudden death. Heartworm disease can be prevented by daily or monthly doses of appropriate medications. Before beginning any medication, your dog must obtain a blood test to insure he is negative for the disease.

Consult your veterinarian as to the wisdom of using monthly preparations that contain the drug ivermectin. Some Boxers are extremely sensitive to it, and I personally know of one death as a result. Many Boxer owners elect to use the monthly preventative called Interceptor, which does not contain ivermectin. Manufacturers still supply the one-a-day heartworm preventive pills that were the mainstay of prevention until the monthly doses were developed. I continue to give the once daily medication to my own dogs. In areas of the country where mosquitoes are a constant problem, veterinarians advise that dogs should be kept on heartworm preventives year-round.

Coccidia: Coccidia are protozoan parasites living in the intestines. They most commonly affect puppies who eat contaminated soil or feces. Symptoms include loose stools with mucous and blood, emaciation and dehydration. Proper sanitation is critical, and certain sulfa drugs are curative. The spores of coccidiosis (oocytes) thrive in moist, unsanitary environments. However, they may also live in common garden soil, and a coccidia infection is not necessarily indicative of poor husbandry. Oocytes are shed intermittently in the feces, so several fecal examinations may be necessary before a positive diagnosis is made.

Giardia: This protozoal disease affects mammals and birds. The ingestion of contaminated water is the most common means of infection. The parasites live in the small intestine and are transmitted in the feces of the host. Symptoms include chronic diarrhea, which may be intermittent, as well as weight loss. The feces tend to be pale and contain mucous. Giardia infestations are either on the rise or being more commonly diagnosed than in prior years.

EXTERNAL PARASITES

As if we didn't have enough to worry about with all the internal parasites that can affect our dogs, we have several external parasites just waiting to make a meal of them. Luckily, these do respond to topical and systemic treatment, but as with all treatments, it is important to be very careful and follow all of your veterinarian's instructions.

The Ubiquitous Flea

The annoying, persistent and fast-multiplying flea is a bloodsucking insect. It carries disease and acts as an intermediate host to the tapeworm. It can jump great distances and readily attaches itself to a host if one is nearby. Fleas need moisture and warmth to grow and reproduce; therefore, in seasonal climates they often do not pose a problem during the winter. In tropical climates or in heated interiors, they can be a problem all year long.

Flea bites cause local irritations. Hence, your dog will scratch in an attempt to rid himself of these parasites. Some dogs are allergic to the saliva in flea bites and develop an acute hypersensitivity to fleas. They scratch constantly and may develop an acute dermatitis. Fortunately, the Boxer is not prone to such reactions.

Fleas are prodigious multipliers and may seem to be everywhere. Female fleas lay eggs that drop off and hatch into larvae resembling worms. These will grow into adult fleas. Unchecked, they may make your dog miserable—and will readily attack *you* if you send your dog on a vacation.

Fleas are easy to see. They look like small, dark, moving specks. If the infection is slight, you may see only flea dirt on your Boxer's short coat—tiny specks that look like bits of dirt but are really flea feces. If you moisten flea dirt, the water will become tinged with red because it contains blood. Common sites of infestation are at the scrotum and around and under the tail. In severe infections, fleas can be found almost anywhere on the dog.

There are no easy solutions to controlling fleas. In addition to the dog, his environment must be treated. All of the following options can be employed, and often a combination is required: insecticidal shampoos, soaps and powders for the dog; foggers, sprays or bombs (preferably containing insect growth regulators to prevent the larvae from developing into mature insects) for the environment; soaps and powders. Diatomaceous earth, which contains sharp particles that mutilate the larvae, can be spread in the yard or kennel quarters. This is a natural and safe preventive, but almost

After walks in wooded areas or in high grass, it is especially important to check your dogs for ticks. (P. Billhardt)

all flea products contain certain toxic chemicals and must be used with caution. So-called natural preparations may be equally toxic. The newer Frontline and other "drops" products may be effective but must be used under the supervision of a veterinarian. Indeed it is wise to consult your veterinarian for professional advice, and pay particular attention to treatments for young puppies. We do not find flea collars to be effective for adults and contraindicated for puppies.

Ticks

Like fleas, ticks are bloodsucking parasites. They are discouragingly hardy and are carriers of many diseases, including Rocky Mountain Spotted Fever, Lyme Disease and Ehrlichiosis. They are found outdoors in high grass and wooded areas and are quite adept at finding your dog if he walks nearby. They can attach themselves anywhere on your dog, but they have a preference for soft tissue, especially the insides of the ears. You may notice them if your Boxer seems to be scratching at one particular site. In addition, many Boxers have a skin sensitivity to the tick bite, and you may see swelling at the site of attachment; it's usually easy to spot on the short, smooth coat.

You can remove a tick with tweezers or pull it out with your fingers. Grasp the tick as close to the dog's skin as possible and pull straight out so as not to leave behind the tick's head. Swab the area with disinfectant, and wash your own hands thoroughly. Never attempt to burn a tick with a match.

Tick season can be any time the temperature is above freezing but is often considered to be spring and fall. During tick season, you should do a daily exam for ticks on your dog. Tick-control products are available for the dog and his environment, but always consult your veterinarian before using these preparations. They may be too toxic for your Boxer.

Ticks are responsible for spreading Lyme Disease, which is now widespread throughout the United States. It is caused by a spirochete, *Borrelia Burgdorferi,* and is transmitted by a variety of ticks that infest rodents and deer. Symptoms usually appear as soon as a few days to a few weeks after the initial bite. They include depression, low-grade and occasionally high-grade fevers, lack of appetite, swelling of joints and often severe pain in the limbs and spine. The pain may migrate from one site to another.

Individual cases don't necessarily include all symptoms, which makes Lyme Disease difficult to diagnose and often causes it to be mistaken for other conditions. Your veterinarian must be alert to the possibility of Lyme in your area and take appropriate treatment measures, which include blood testing for the disease. However, a negative test result does not necessarily mean Lyme can be ruled out. Specific antibiotic therapy early in the course of the disease will cure most cases of Lyme quite quickly, but misdiagnosis and delay in treatment can lead to cardiac and neurological complications, which can prove fatal. Unfortunately, once cured, your Boxer can be reinfected by another tick carrying Lyme disease, as no immunity results from the initial exposure or treatment. Preventive vaccination against the disease is now available, but it has a rather short-lived period of effectiveness in many cases.

MEDICAL CONDITIONS AFFECTING THE BOXER

Despite breeders' best efforts, Boxers do occasionally suffer from conditions to which the breed seems to be predisposed. They may be genetic in origin or occasioned by environmental influences. In many instances, diagnosis and treatment will affect a cure or symptomatic relief.

Hip Dysplasia

Hip Dysplasia is a developmental disease of the hip joint that affects many breeds of dogs. The head of the femur (thigh bone) and the acetabulum (hip socket) become incompatible; the joint weakens and loses proper function. Reluctance to engage in strenuous physical activity, lameness and pain are all possible signs of dysplasia, usually manifested between the ages of 4 months to 1 year. Stair climbing and rising from a prone or sitting position may also be painful, and the dog may cry out if the hip joint is manipulated.

Radiographs are definitively diagnostic and will show evidence of abnormal joint laxity. Treatment is aimed at relieving symptoms of pain and includes drug therapy and surgery. Hip dysplasia is thought to be hereditary, but other factors such as diet and conditioning cannot be ruled out. Dogs older than 2 years can have their radiographs evaluated and may be registered free of the disease by the Orthopedic Foundation for Animals (OFA) in Columbia, Missouri. Dogs are rated Fair, Good and Excellent. It is important to understand that any of these ratings certifies the dog is free of hip dysplasia. (See Chapter 12.)

Osteochondritis

During periods of maximal growth, usually between 4 and 8 months, your Boxer could show signs of osteochondritis, or OCD. This is a condition that causes faulty formation of cartilage on the heads of the long bones in the shoulders or stifles. In Boxers, it is most commonly seen in the shoulder. Lameness and stiffness are symptomatic in the young animal.

Trauma is a likely cause, as well as excessive supplementation of vitamins and minerals to the growing puppy. Our dogs receive no supplementation to their nutritionally complete diet. Afflicted dogs respond well to crate rest over a period of weeks. More serious cases may require surgery, but the prognosis is usually good. In a fast-growing breed such as the Boxer, we advocate feeding the extra-high-protein puppy foods only through the age of 4 months, at which time we switch to adult formulations.

Hypothyroidism (Thyroid Deficiency)

The onset of hypothyroidism in the adult Boxer is becoming more commonly diagnosed. The condition may be caused by thyroid tumors or a primary malfunction of the thyroid, resulting in a deficiency of thyroid hormones. The deficient thyroid may have an effect on many organ systems, including the heart. Symptoms may include excessive hair thinning and loss, obesity, anemia, reproductive failures, infertility and lethargy. Sometimes a dog may have inadequate thyroid levels without any overt physical symptoms at all. Diagnosis is confirmed by testing the blood and detecting inadequate levels of circulating thyroid hormones, T3 and T4. The administration of carefully determined oral doses of replacement hormone will alleviate most symptoms and will probably need to be given for the remainder of the dog's life.

Cancers

Boxers are at risk for a variety of tumors. These include benign skin tumors (lipomas and histiocytomas) as well as cancers affecting the brain, skin, thyroid, mammary glands, testes, heart, lymphatic system, pancreas and other organs. Benign skin tumors usually need either no treatment or simple surgical excision under local anesthesia. Histiocytomas, resembling pink buttons, usually resolve themselves over a period of several months. The application of iodine speeds their healing.

Malignancies require treatment specific to the cancer itself and vary widely. As in humans with cancer, dogs are treated with surgery, chemotherapy and sometimes radiation. Tremendous advances have been made in treatment protocols and survival times, but unfortunately there is no way to predict whether or not your Boxer will develop cancer in his lifetime. However, it is prudent to be alert to any unusual growths or medical developments, especially as your Boxer ages. Consult with your veterinarian immediately if you notice anything suspicious.

Gingival Hyperplasia

Gingival hyperplasias are benign tumors of the mouth, mainly an overgrowth of gum tissue, commonly seen in middle-aged and older Boxers. These tumors may be numerous, but they usually cause no significant harm. Occasionally, they distort the placement of the lips and are cosmetically unattractive. If they are especially bothersome, they may bleed and actually cause a malocclusion. Since they can catch and hold food particles, you must pay special attention to oral hygiene. It is wise to consult your veterinarian to rule out any potentially serious oral malignancy. Surgery will effectively remove the excessive gum tissue, but the

tissue unfortunately has a tendency to grow back. Laser removal techniques are being developed that may prove beneficial.

Demodectic Mange

There are two kinds of mange that affect canines in North America: sarcoptic mange, which is highly contagious and causes intense itching, and demodectic mange. Demodectic mange may cause nothing more than a few localized areas of mild hair loss, or it infrequently may progress to a generalized pustular form that in very rare instances can kill the dog. Both forms of the disease are caused by different microscopic mites that burrow into the hair follicles and epidermis. These mites are transmitted by close contact and, in puppies, most often by exposure to their infected mother. While sarcoptic mange can usually be cured by appropriate topical treatment, demodectic mange in the Boxer sometimes remains stubborn and resistant to all manner of preparations designed to eradicate it—both topical and internal. Overtreatment can actually exacerbate the condition. Be sure not to overdo it, and follow whatever protocols your veterinarian establishes. The status of the immune system of your Boxer may predict how readily he will respond to treatment. It is also thought that a breach of the immune system is what enables the common demodectic mange mite to cause clinical symptoms in the first place. Mild demodectic mange is sometimes seen in the growing puppy or at particular periods of stress in the adolescent. Usually, it will subside when the dog reaches maturity.

Pyoderma (Pyogenic Dermatitis and Acne)

Pyoderma is an infection of the skin, either superficial or deep. Superficial lesions appear as small pustules, often on the dog's face and chin. Deeper lesions include draining cysts between the toes. Some Boxers are prone to these annoying and unsightly infections, most often caused by bacteria. I find that they are more common among adolescents and gradually lessen or disappear with age. There is some suggestion that immune deficiencies or allergies in certain Boxers may predispose them to these conditions. Most superficial lesions resolve with topical treatment—soaps and antibacterial baths. Deeper infections, such as those resulting from interdigital nodules (cysts between the toes), usually require antibiotic treatment and warmwater soaking of the affected limb to encourage the cysts to drain. Such nodules, sometimes fostered by foreign bodies in the form of hairs and grains of sand, are often painful to the dog until they are resolved. They occasionally recur.

Heart Disease

Like most breeds of dogs, Boxers are subject to heart ailments. These include congenital anomalies as well as acquired disease later in life. Boxer heart disease usually falls into two important categories: aortic stenosis and cardiomyopathy.

Aortic Stenosis

This is a congenital condition, a narrowing or constriction of the outflow tract from the left ventricle to the aorta. Usually, this defect occurs below the aortic valve and thus is referred to as subaortic stenosis (SAS). It can be detected as a systolic murmur by your veterinarian in young puppies and older dogs. Sometimes the murmur will not show up until the dog reaches a certain physical size and the constriction becomes evident.

This murmur must be distinguished from other types of murmurs—often so-called innocent flow murmurs that disappear as the puppy grows. There is no practical surgical treatment, and if the condition results in arrhythmias, antiarrhythmic therapy is usually instituted. SAS can cause heart failure and sudden death, but mild forms of the anomaly may go undetected and are not incompatible with a normal life span. There is strong evidence to suggest that this condition is hereditary. Doppler echocardiograms are valuable in assessing the degree of any stenosis should one exist. They measure the velocity of aortic blood flow in the area of a suspected stricture. An ongoing study in Britain rates as acceptable for breeding any Boxer with blood velocity via Doppler echocardiography less than 2.0, with an audible murmur of Grade 2 or below. However, controversy exists as to whether "gray area" animals should be considered as afflicted with SAS and therefore unwise to use for breeding.

Cardiomyopathy

This is perhaps the most frustrating disease to which the Boxer may succumb. It is an electrical-conduction disturbance, a condition of the heart muscle itself causing erroneous electrical impulses

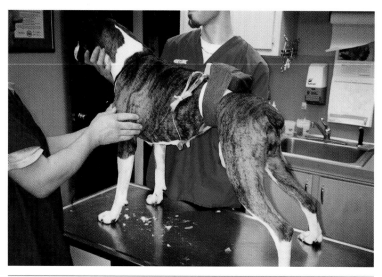

A 6-year-old Boxer is fitted with a Holter Monitor to check for arrhythmia, which may be indicative of cardiomyopathy. (C. Baldwin, DVM)

Cardiomyopathy is widespread throughout the breed in North America, and there are no easy ways to avoid it. The good news is that your Boxer may never develop this condition. Nonetheless, you must be aware of its symptoms. If your Boxer ever displays sudden weakness or faints, you must investigate the cause of these behaviors. They are classic cardiomyopathy signs that must not be ignored, even if your dog seems to recover almost immediately. Often, even if you take your dog to your veterinarian after such an episode, the heart may have reverted to an entirely normal rhythm. Unfortunately, this is no guarantee of a healthy heart because arrhythmia, usually ventricular in the Boxer, may

to disrupt the heart's normal rhythm. This arrhythmia often leads to sudden death or heart failure resulting in death. Histological studies at necropsy often reveal the presence of fatty infiltrations in the heart muscle tissue—a consistent finding in Boxer cardiomyopathy. Arrhythmias can be brought on by certain poisons; bacterial, parasitic and viral infections (notably parvovirus); severe uremia; diabetes and heatstroke. However, in Boxers they most often occur in middle age (and sometimes at disturbingly young ages) due to no known cause; unfortunately, heredity probably plays a key role. Boxer breeders the world over are terribly frustrated that there is at present no way to diagnose the propensity for this condition in asymptomatic breeding animals. Therefore, the disease passes on from one generation to the next.

only be detected intermittently or upon stress in the early stages of the disease. More sophisticated testing is required. One of the most informative tests involves the wearing of a twenty-four-hour Holter Monitor. This noninvasive device will record your dog's heartbeat and rhythm long enough for abnormalities to be detected if they are present.

Cardiomyopathy can be treated with appropriate antiarrhythmic drugs, and once your dog's heart has been properly regulated, he may live on for years with no further symptoms. Conscientious Boxer breeders who support the American Boxer Charitable Foundation are funding several research projects investigating this devastating disease, hoping one day to identify genetic markers so that cardiomyopathy can either be eliminated or greatly reduced in the breed so that we do not lose our dogs before they have a chance to grow old.

Torsion and Bloat

Deep-chested dogs such as the Boxer are sometimes subject to bloat. This condition may progress into a life-threatening emergency. The stomach distends with gas, food and air, and you may notice that your Boxer's abdomen suddenly looks very full and abnormally large. The dog may whine, salivate and make unsuccessful attempts to vomit. Unfortunately this distension often causes the stomach to twist on its axis (torsion), shutting off the circulation. Shock and death follow without surgical intervention. In simple bloat, without torsion, the gaseous buildup can be relieved by the passage of a stomach tube to release the pressure.

Bloat and torsion are often associated with the rapid ingestion of a large meal or too much water, and vigorous exercise before or after eating and drinking. However, some dogs develop this condition for entirely unknown reasons. It is prudent to feed your Boxer two meals a day so that he does not eat a huge quantity of food at any one time. We usually restrict exercise for about one hour after a meal. The frantic gulping of food, which necessitates the ingestion of large amounts of air, should be discouraged. If you have any suspicion that your Boxer may be in the early stages of bloat, no matter what time of day or night, proceed immediately to the nearest veterinarian or emergency clinic qualified to perform the surgery and aftercare that is so critical to your dog's survival. It is a wise breeder who determines ahead of time, before a frantic emergency, whom he or she will call at 4 A.M. to save his dog's life. Minutes count.

EMERGENCY RESUSCITATION

If your Boxer is in danger of dying due to suffocation or if he has stopped breathing, you may be the only person at hand who can help to revive him. To that end, you would be wise to learn canine CPR—cardiopulmonary resuscitation. Hopefully, you will never need to use it. Here is what you should do:

1. Clear the airway. Wipe mucous from the mouth and nose. Draw the tongue forward. If the dog has inhaled water, put him in a position so that his head and neck hang vertically; you are trying to drain fluids from his lungs and respiratory passages. If you cannot lift him, lay him on his side so that his head is lower than his body.

2. Place both hands, one on top of the other, over the region of the heart—where the elbow meets the ribs. Compress the chest by making vigorous downward thrusts, about 100 compressions per minute. This is strenuous work. Check for a heartbeat about every thirty seconds. If you should get a pulse, your next efforts should be directed at reestablishing respiration.

Checking for a Pulse

The easiest way to check to see whether or not the heart is beating is by feeling for the femoral

Here, a fit, athletic Boxer, Ch. Bellcrest's Just Watch Me, helps with his owners' skiing technique. (S. Bell)

arterial pulse on the inside of the upper part of your Boxer's rear legs. If you move your index finger down the femur (upper bone) and apply slight pressure, you should be able to feel a pulse if it is present.

Artificial Respiration

Exhaled air contains about 16 percent oxygen. This small amount is enough to sustain life in both people and dogs. Although the Boxer's short muzzle and nasal passages present special difficulties, you can perform mouth-to-muzzle breathing by closing the muzzle with one hand, placing your mouth over your dog's nostrils and exhaling. Watch your dog's chest: If he is getting air into his lungs, you will see a slight rise and fall as you breathe the air into him. Administering ten to fifteen rapid thrusts (as in "Emergency Respiration" above) and one deep breath—repeated until help arrives or you can get to a veterinarian—will give your dog a chance. If his chest does not rise and fall and the nasal passages are blocked, try sealing the nose and breathing directly into the mouth. Your task will be much easier if two people are available—one to perform CPR and one to employ artificial respiration.

These tasks are physically demanding—it is genuinely hard labor. But do not despair and do not give up until about fifteen to twenty minutes have passed with no favorable response.

HAPPINESS IS . . .

Although I have discussed many situations and conditions that may be injurious to your Boxer, it is important to remember that he probably will enjoy robust good health until age catches up with him. It is simply prudent to be aware of proper health protocols, and to note the diseases or syndromes that are unique to the Boxer. Every breed of dog has its genetic heritage, and that includes predisposition to certain ills. The wise owner will prepare for the worst but anticipate the best. Most often, efforts to keep a Boxer happy and healthy will be rewarded by a dog who brings happiness and joy for many years.

(E. Mangiafico)

Routine Care of Your Boxer

The old adage "You are what you eat" applies to dogs as well as people. Your Boxer's daily diet is reflected in the spring of his step, the condition of his coat and his overall outlook on life. You cannot "groom" superb condition—it comes after months of careful attention to diet, exercise and overall husbandry. However, you can control the success or failure of the routines you establish, and one of the biggest favors you can do for your dog is to put the proper type and quantity of food into his bowl. Do not skimp on quality in order to save a few dollars—the investment you make in the best of dog foods will repay you many times over. Your dog will spend less time at the veterinarian's office; he will win more often in hot competition; and he will be a happier pet in your home.

BASIC NUTRITION

There are six staples of nutrition required by dogs every day: protein, carbohydrates, fats, vitamins, minerals and water. Commercial dog food manufacturers spend millions of dollars to ensure that their foods are nutritionally complete—that they contain the proper amounts of each nutrient category (except water, which you must provide) to sustain healthy growth and maintenance.

WHAT TO FEED YOUR PUPPY

Although you will initially follow the breeder's advice, you will eventually settle on a diet of your own choosing for your Boxer. Availability of various brand names may influence your choice. However, the best barometer of what to feed your growing Boxer is the puppy himself. Is he healthy? Does his coat shine? Is he robust and happy? If so, you must be on the right track.

Chow time! These 6-week-old pups eat from a cleverly designed puppy pan. (V. Jaeger)

weight. Therefore, the first item on the list makes up the heaviest volume. If you see lamb or chicken first on the list, don't be mislead: Remember that meat contains up to 75 percent moisture, so it may make up only a small fraction of the entire food. The label will list every component in the kibble, including minerals, vitamins and preservatives. It will also give you the "Guaranteed Analysis"—percentages of protein, fat, fiber and moisture contained in the food.

About Kibble

The mainstay of your puppy's diet, and indeed his adult diet, is the dry food or "kibble" that you feed. There are dazzling displays of kibbled dog food in every supermarket, pet emporium and feed store. Be sure to investigate the brands carried by the supermarket, but do not ignore the so-called designer brands that may only be available in more specialized stores. They are usually more expensive but may actually prove more economical in the long run if they offer your Boxer better health.

When choosing a brand name, you must learn to read and understand a packaging label. Label ingredients are listed in descending order by

We prefer to feed dry food that is naturally, not chemically, preserved. There is some controversy regarding potential ill effects from the preservative ethoxyquin, and we choose not to feed kibble that contains it.

Labels can be misleading, and no reference is made to the actual nutritional value of the ingredients. Nor will you know if the percentage of protein, for example, is made up of chicken meat or chicken feathers. Yes, some dog food companies use feathers, beaks, hooves and horns to achieve certain protein levels. Direct inquiries to dog food manufacturers may prove enlightening to a degree. The success of experienced breeders feeding a particular brand may prove the best barometer of success in the long run. Presently, according to the

American Association of Feed Control Officials (AAFCO), recommended percentages per pound of food for growth are crude protein 19.8 percent and crude fat 7.2 percent. You will find that most good brands of quality kibble exceed these requirements. In fact, my own chosen brand of puppy food contains 32 percent protein and 21 percent fat. The amount of food you give to your puppy depends on the nutritional and caloric content of the food. Manufacturers usually label their kibble with suggestions per pound of your puppy's body weight. I find that the amounts recommended are often in excess of what we feed.

FOOD AMOUNTS AND REGIMENS

If I fed my adults or puppies the amounts of food recommended on many bags or cans of dog food, I'd be sure to have some of the fattest boxers in town! Remember, it is the manufacturer's goal to sell you more food, so do be careful not to overfeed. Calorie contents also differ, sometimes markedly, from kibble to kibble and can to can. The following are some general recommendations and observations.

Two to Four Months

In general, we feed a growing Boxer puppy from 8 to 16 weeks of age between 3 and 4 cups of kibble daily. Of course, this amount will vary considerably with the individual puppy's metabolism, his rate of activity and the amount of any additional foods in his diet. Use your eyes and your common sense to make necessary judgments. Your puppy should not

be fat, but rather lean and well muscled, with his hip bones covered and only the slightest suggestion of ribs showing under his glossy coat. If you are looking at an animal in optimum condition, then you are feeding appropriate foods.

Make sure that your growing Boxer pups are getting enough nutrition.
(S. Abraham)

We always feed kibble mixed with warm water. We begin this practice at weaning and continue it throughout the dog's life. I have always believed that soaked kibble promotes better digestibility and less susceptibility to torsion. In addition to water, we add a small amount of canned food or chopped meat to enhance palatability. But remember that the greatest nutritional value comes from the kibble, not the can! While you could, theoretically, feed your dog nothing but canned food, it is much more economical to use dry food as a mainstay. The latter also promotes a firmer stool and, therefore, easier cleanup.

At this age, feeding three times daily is adequate for your puppy's needs. In fact, if you work and cannot get home to prepare a midday meal, your puppy will not starve. Just feed morning and evening, with perhaps a small snack before bedtime. Be sure to provide your puppy with plenty of fresh water. This is essential because inadequate water intake can damage his kidneys or cause dehydration. Your dog's body is made up of over 66 percent water, and it needs to be continually renewed.

Your Boxer puppy will thrive on a regular routine of feeding and exercise. Do not continually change the routine at this age—you are trying to establish good eating habits, and these are learned, not necessarily inherited from his mother. If you feed in a crate, always feed in a crate. If you feed in the kitchen, let the puppy always expect his food in the kitchen. Whatever else you do, do not let the puppy train *you*, because he may be very adept at it.

Not all Boxer pups clean up their bowls. They may wander off, eat a mouthful, then retire to the TV room to chew on a bone. The easily distracted puppy is one reason why I prefer to feed inside a crate, where the puppy's mind is more likely to concentrate on his kibble. If he does not eat all of his food, you should still remove the bowl after about thirty minutes. And he should not fill up on treats while he awaits his next meal. My mother still tells the story of our first Boxer, who was so

indulged by us as a puppy that he ate very little dog food at all. He once spit a mouthful of prime rib onto the floor; he would have trained us to feed him caviar before we got wise and decided dog food would be *it*, thank you!

Six to Twelve Months

A puppy is officially considered such by the American Kennel Club until he reaches 12 months of age. If you elect to show him, he is eligible to compete in Puppy classes from 6 to 12 months. During that time, he is not only growing taller, but is also beginning to fill out and develop muscle. When your Boxer reaches 10 to 12 months, he will be close to his adult height, though not his mature adult weight. Some dogs mature early, some late—just like people.

Feeding the rapidly growing and maturing puppy presents special challenges. You must adjust his food quantity as his condition dictates, although it won't be terribly different than the total consumed by the younger pup. Sooner or later, someone is going to ask you what vitamin-mineral supplement you are using. We do not supplement our puppies with pills, capsules or powder forms, or by any artificial means whatsoever. It is our belief that we can do much more harm than good by tampering with the carefully formulated ingredients in the food we have so carefully selected. While common sense may tell us that a puppy's bones need calcium for optimal growth and development, please understand that the kibble itself is sufficient to satisfy these needs. Altering the balance of calcium and phosphorous via so-called calcium supplements may be harmful and cause bone and joint abnormalities such as osteochondritis or oteodystrophy. At the same time, it is certainly beneficial during puppyhood as well as adulthood to add calcium-rich natural foods to your dog's diet, such as plain yogurt or cottage cheese. Just be sure not to overdo it—a couple of spoonfuls at a meal are quite sufficient.

When the puppy reaches 6 months of age, or even a month sooner, we switch him from puppy food to the adult food that he will eat for the rest of his life. He no longer needs the extra-high-protein formulations of younger puppyhood, and, in fact, the extra protein can predispose him to problems related to overstimulation of his growth. The adult kibble I feed contains 23 percent protein and 14 percent fat; yours may differ, but is likely to approximate these levels.

FEEDING THE ADULT BOXER

An adult Boxer should do well on two feedings a day. (S. Bell)

A Boxer should do well on a twice-a-day feeding schedule—whatever times work best with your schedule. Our adults eat approximately 2 cups of food per meal. No more! Feeding twice daily is healthier and less likely to result in bloat or other less-serious digestive abnormalities. Why fill the dog's relatively small stomach with one huge meal? If dogs are left to self-feeding plans, they learn to eat small amounts frequently. That is natural for them. So feeding every twelve hours or so more closely approximates the dog's natural regimen. Contrary to the layman's opinion, Boxers are not naturally gassy dogs if they are being fed properly. Excessive flatulence would be a sign that the dog food might need changing.

If you decide to change the brand of kibble you are feeding, be sure to do it gradually. Feed the new food mixed with the old in ever smaller proportions until the change is complete. Your dog's digestive system needs time to assimilate the nutritional changes of one food to another. If you do it all at once, loose stools or diarrhea may result. Likewise, when traveling, try to take water from home with you because abrupt water changes can also predispose your Boxer to the same loose stools. Both tap and well waters can vary markedly in chemical composition from household to household.

If your dog misses a meal or for some reason is deprived of a meal, he may get a digestive stomach upset and vomit small amounts of yellow, frothy semiliquid material. This is not an uncommon occurrence in the Boxer. Do not be concerned; just offer him his meal when appropriate, perhaps coaxing him with a bit of chopped meat or a dog biscuit, and all will be well.

It may be appropriate to point out that the dog is an omnivore; that is, he eats both animal and vegetable matter. Even the wolf and the wild dog of Africa demonstrate this fact by first eating the stomachs and intestines of the herbivores who make up the bulk of their prey. Balance in proportion between animal and vegetable matter in the domesticated dog's diet is the key to success in raising a healthy dog, whether it be a Boxer or one of his predacious wild cousins. If you maintain your Boxer on scientifically formulated and balanced foods, supply him with plenty of fresh water and take care not to overfeed, you are likely to have a healthy dog who ages gracefully and looks younger than his years.

EAR CROPPING, TAIL DOCKING AND DEWCLAW REMOVAL

In the United States at the present time, Boxer ears, tails and dewclaws are usually cropped, docked and removed, respectively. Indeed, in 1998, the American Boxer Club voted not to include a description of the natural ear in the breed standard when parity with the cropped ear was sought by a vocal minority.

Tail docking is customarily performed at between 3 and 5 days of age, depending on the size and vigor of the puppy. Topical novocaine can be administered to even a very young pup at tail-docking time. The procedure is so brief that many veterinarians use no painkilling medication. There are many docking techniques, but all are aimed at a cosmetically attractive result. A useful gauge of the proper length to cut a tail is to take a common U.S. nickel (5-cent coin), place it gently on the underside of the tail resting at the anus and

There are many tail-docking techniques, but all are aimed toward a cosmetically attractive result. (S. Abraham)

ask the veterinarian to make the cut at the place where the nickel ends. When the practitioner is finished with his work, the tail should be approximately ¾ inch long when measured underneath.

Dewclaws (found on the front legs) are removed at the same time as tails are docked. They are simply snipped off, and they heal rapidly. If they are not removed, they can snag and pull in the active adult, causing pain and bleeding.

Ears are usually cropped at between 6 and 12 weeks, the age being determined by the preferences of the veterinarian who performs the procedure. Some like to work with more ear length, and some with less. Most states require that a licensed veterinarian do the surgery, although there are non-licensed laypeople who

Ears are usually cropped when a puppy is between 6 and 12 weeks old. The ears are then "trained" with rigid supports wrapped in surgical tape. (S. Abraham)

in young puppies. It is common for ear surgery to be performed with the use of inhalant anesthetics rather than injectables that may be more difficult to reverse if any complications arise.

Occasionally, local anesthetics alone are used by a few practitioners. Pain is therefore not an issue during the actual surgery. However, the healing process, which takes approximately two weeks, can cause some discomfort, especially if a litter of pups is housed together and their play is not always mindful of each other's tender ears. Breeders strive to minimize any roughhousing during this period. Most Boxers will come through the procedure beautifully, with no traumatic aftereffects.

Ear care, and taping after healing is complete, is

have trained in this work and are quite competent. Breeders should check their local state regulations. The breeder should be well acquainted with the skill of the individual practitioner, with particular attention paid to his or her expertise with anesthesia

an art and a skill that all of us are capable of learning. However, it is not only helpful but almost a necessity that the novice owner or breeder be mentored by someone experienced in taping methodology. Some dogs have ears that stand perfectly after only a few tapings, and others may take multiple tapings over many months—even more than a year. The most common cause of ear "failure to stand" is owners giving up too soon—often just when taping will do the most good in the adolescent.

While it is not in the scope of this book to discuss every taping method, a few hints may be helpful. First, when taping, use a good-quality surgical adhesive tape, the kind often found in medical pharmacies. We use 1-inch-wide Johnson & Johnson Zonas tape. Some kennel supply houses also provide excellent-quality surgical adhesive in their catalogs. The waterproof adhesive tapes commonly available in supermarkets and many drugstores are too harsh on the Boxer's delicate ear tissue. If you must use that tape, be sure to wrap it over a surgical adhesive so the tape is not touching the ear itself. It is wise to buy an adhesive remover so the tape will not pull and cause distress to your dog when you need to remove it. Many breeders use surgical liquid adhesive (Skin-Bond) to affix Molefoam (used to cushion toes of the human foot) or ⅜-inch backer rod (used to caulk windows) to the inside of the ear, molded to its shape. This has the advantage of using little or no tape and, therefore, minimizes any discomfort due to pulling when the tape is removed. Other breeders prefer the more conventional taping procedure that often uses "stays" in the ears to give them strength— Tampax tubes or tubes made of rolled paper towels. Everyone has his or her pet methods, and there is always a new technique to try. Whatever your technique, it is important not to let the ears tip in toward the center of the head during the healing

It is important to minimize roughhousing right after ear cropping. Once the ears are healed, it's back to play. (D. Merolla)

Ivy's natural ears have a life of their own prior to cropping. (S. Abraham)

and taping process. This may cause the ears to assume such an unnatural posture as a permanent attitude, and taping them erect becomes more problematic.

Tail docking and ear cropping are controversial procedures in the minds of many people, in that they see them as largely cosmetic elective surgeries. This can be argued ad infinitum. Despite the efforts of so-called animal rights groups, tradition and the preference for the noble look imparted by the erect ear have insured that humane docking and cropping are going to continue in the foreseeable future in the United States.

GROOMING THE BOXER

As you might imagine, grooming the Boxer is not a complicated event. Affectionately referred to as "wash-and-wear-dogs," Boxers require no complex efforts in order to look clean and neat. Nonetheless, the vigilant owner may use his grooming time to observe his dog carefully for any signs of injury or disease—fleas, ticks, skin tumors, thinning coat, wounds and so on.

A grooming table is a great help. It is usually made with a sturdy, nonskid surface and metal legs. You may fold it up for ease of storage when you are traveling with your dog on the show circuit. Such a table, available through kennel supply houses and some pet shops, will place

This pup is an obvious argument for early and effective ear taping. (S. Abraham)

A grooming table is a big help in preventing back strain as you groom your Boxer. (S. Abraham)

BATHING AND BRUSHING

A Boxer's coat is short and sleek. It is also unbelievably tenacious, as it successfully clings to upholstered furniture, rugs and clothing. Your Boxer will shed slightly but with some regularity, especially if you live in a climate with dramatic seasonal changes. Therefore, a currycomb made of firm rubber, used in a circular motion, will rid your dog of dead hair and save the furniture. Here in the Northeast, I find that our Boxers shed winter coats just in time to look moth-eaten for the big spring dog shows! At that time, a currycomb is a must. A soft-bristle brush can also be used, but it won't be as effective as the currycomb for removing unwanted hair. Remember that the Boxer has normally sensitive skin, so any brushing should be done gently and with care.

Your Boxer does not need frequent bathing. As I mentioned before, he helps to keep himself polished and tidy by licking himself clean. Usually, your Boxer's front paws will be kept spotless—that's the easiest place for his tongue to reach. Do not bathe your Boxer too frequently, because doing so can remove essential oils from your dog's skin, can result in irritation and may dry out his coat. We bathe our dogs only when they are going to be shown or when they have done something unmentionable, such as rolling in a nice pile of deer dung.

Minor surface dirt can easily be brushed away or spot-cleaned with mild soap and water on a soft glove or washcloth. If a complete bath is required, we wet the dog thoroughly with warm water, then apply shampoo and gently rub it over the entire coat, taking care that it does not get into the dog's

Ch. Trefoil's Choirmaster, bathed, trimmed and ready for the ring. (S. Abraham)

your dog at eye level so that you can have easy access to him. It will save you backaches and eyestrain over the years. A metal arm with a noose can clamp to the table, affording you more control over your dog when he is being groomed. However, be sure not to leave him alone with his head in the restraint lest he choose that moment to vacate the premises!

eyes or ears. I usually start at the rear and work forward to the head. Be sure to keep your Boxer warm through any bathing process, as he can easily become chilled. When the dog is completely soaped, we rinse him *very* thoroughly. Shampoo residue can cause skin irritation and unsightly soap "flakes" to appear; rinse very, very well.

If you must bathe your puppy, be sure that he is protected from drafts. (E. DeGroff)

Although you can give baths indoors (and of necessity in the winter), we prefer to bathe our dogs outside on a warm day, taking care that the water temperature is constant and comfortable. Water can be carried in a bucket or sprayed from the garden hose. If you use a hose, remember that water initially warmed by the sun as it sits in the hose can change temperature rapidly as you demand more water from the well or town supply. While your Boxer will vigorously shake himself to rid his coat of the rinse water, you should still dry your Boxer thoroughly using clean, soft toweling. Then let the sun finish the process.

SHAMPOOS

There are almost as many dog shampoos as there are dogs. There are oatmeal shampoos, tea tree shampoos, moisturizing shampoos, whitening shampoos, anti-inflammatory shampoos and a plethora of flea shampoos. Conditioners are not necessary with the Boxer's short coat. If you are bathing to kill fleas, it's important to choose a soap that is not too toxic to your dog. Remember that even the so-called natural ingredients may contain deadly poisons in tiny doses. Always read the label on any shampoo carefully, and use only as instructed. Most flea products should not be used on young puppies; read the manufacturer's instructions carefully. We prefer to use a pyrethrin-based flea shampoo when necessary, as we find it to be mild, safe and effective. (Pyrethrin is a product of ground chrysanthemums.) Unlike other shampoos, flea soaps should be left on the dog for several minutes to be sure that they kill the resident flea population.

TRIMMING TOENAILS

Regular trimming of your Boxer's toenails is essential to his well-being. Untrimmed nails lead to splayed toes and feet, and will cause your dog to slip on smooth surfaces. They also look awful. If you begin gentle trimming on your young puppy, you should have no trouble continuing to trim throughout your Boxer's life. Your puppy's breeder undoubtedly began to trim his nails from the very earliest weeks in the whelping box, so hopefully your puppy will already know the routine.

Be sure not to cut into the quick of the toenail, as that area is very sensitive. (S. Abraham)

It will help to cut toenails on the grooming table outside on a sunny day. That way, you can hold the nail up to the light and see the small vein that travels about two-thirds the length of the nail. If you cannot see it, trim the nail a bit at a time instead of making one definitive cut. Simply try to avoid cutting too close to that vein. The area is sensitive and your dog will let you know if you get too close—it hurts! In addition to causing real (though brief) pain, cutting too close can result in transient, slight bleeding. If this happens, do not panic—it is not serious. You should have some commercial variant of the familiar styptic powder available, which you can purchase at pet shops, kennel supply shops or your vet's office. Just dip the offending nail into the powder, and the bleeding will stop quickly. It would do so on its own in just a bit more time.

Most dogs do not love to have their nails cut. Therefore, it is important that you maintain control and insist on proceeding. Patience may be required. Soon, nail cutting will be routine to both you and your Boxer and can be accomplished in a few minutes. Nails should be trimmed every couple of weeks, or at least once a month. Show dogs will have their nails trimmed at least once weekly and before every show. It is entirely unnecessary to have your veterinarian maintain your dog's nails—this is definitely a "can do-it-yourself" project.

There are several nail-cutting tools available on the market. One of these is a familiar guillotine type. Another looks like an ordinary scissors designed to fit around the nail. Professionals usually choose an electric grinder—a relatively expensive but marvelous device. Whichever tool you use, be sure that the blades or grinding wheels are changed as necessary.

CLEANING TEETH AND GUMS

Most Boxers do not require regular teeth cleaning. However, it is prudent to check your dog's teeth periodically just to be sure there are no injuries to the enamel or the gums. Your Boxer's mouth should be relatively odorless; if it is smelly, it probably needs attention. Odor usually means that retained or decaying food is caught in the teeth; rarely, an infection may develop. You can gently brush your Boxer's teeth with a soft human toothbrush or a canine brush available at pet supply stores. You can use baking soda and water or one of the commercially available canine toothpastes or mouthwashes. Do not be alarmed if you see an overgrowth of gum tissue in the older Boxer (see "Gingival Hyperplasia" in Chapter 6). This is most probably a benign condition rather common to the breed.

If your Boxer has regular access to hard rubber, nylon or rope chew toys and if he gets occasional biscuit treats, you will usually find that the simple stimulus of chewing will keep his mouth and teeth healthy. Tartar deposits will remain at a minimum. If tartar does develop to any significant degree, you or your vet can remove it by means of a simple dental tool called a tooth scaler. More serious deposits leading to actual tooth decay may (rarely) require a professional cleaning in the vet's office.

EYE CARE

Boxers usually do not need special care of the eyes. However, be careful to keep grooming implements and soaps away from the eyes. Any trauma to the lens can cause corneal abrasion, which in the Boxer can sometimes progress to a more serious ulceration. This can be quite painful. If it occurs, your veterinarian can identify it by staining the cornea and viewing it with an opthalmoscope. Usually, the application of an antibiotic ointment will facilitate healing without complication. Less commonly, a canine opthalmologist with more specialized techniques will be needed to heal the injury (see chapter 12).

GROOMING FOR THE SHOW RING

All the basic grooming techniques just discussed for your house pet apply also to the show dog. However, if you elect to show your Boxer in competitive conformation shows, grooming will take on another dimension. The process will still be simple, but you will have a few more steps to take. First, you should shave the whiskers off the face and under the chin. You will want to use an electric trimmer; we use a small cordless variety that is easy to wield in small spaces. Don't forget the little single hairs that grow out of the black hair dots on the side of the face near the mask. Ears should be shaved as well on the inside and at the base to present a trimmer appearance. In addition, the ear edges should be shaved in one pass with the clippers just to neaten the edge.

The underside of the tail should be shaved and the end hairs trimmed. This step has the added advantage of making the tail just a bit more sensitive to touch, and it will be easier for you or your handler to encourage the tail to stand up in the ring (a desirable feature, according to the current fashion). Any stray hairs should be trimmed from the penile sheath in males. In addition, in both sexes, the hairs on the back of the thighs should be trimmed for neatness. Loin edges and stray belly hairs should likewise be trimmed, and if pasterns need improving, a close shave there may minimize the issue.

So-called chalking of your Boxer is usually done shortly before he enters the ring. Powdered white chalk is applied to the white on his legs and

Ch. Virgo's Market Boomer. (Bill Meyer)

CHAPTER 8

It's Show Time!

A dog show is a showcase—an event held under American Kennel Club rules and regulations, which highlights the achievements of breeders of purebred dogs throughout the country. All dogs are judged against their individual breed Standard, the blueprint for the elusive, so-called perfect dog. The most recent revision of the Boxer Standard was approved by the parent club, the American Boxer Club, in 1989, and was amended slightly in 1999.

Showing your Boxer in the conformation ring should give you a great deal of satisfaction, but it is also a lot of hard work. There is much to learn, many people to meet and friendships to be formed that may last a lifetime. The fraternity of dog show exhibitors is accustomed to rising before dawn, driving long distances and often coming home with nary a ribbon. If you lack persistence, a healthy ego and a certain amount of ambition, then a day at the dog show may not be your idea of fun.

But on almost any given weekend in the United States, there is a dog show going on somewhere. These may be Specialty shows, dedicated to one breed only, or the more common All-Breed show, where all AKC-registered breeds may participate. All the breeds are categorized as belonging to one of seven Groups—Herding, Hound, Non-Sporting, Sporting, Terrier, Toy and Working. The Boxer is in the Working Group—dogs that perform working functions for humans. The Boxer is a guard dog and sometimes a guide dog; the Siberian pulls a sled; the St. Bernard rescues avalanche victims. At the end of the dog show day, the Best of Breed winners in each Group compete in the Group judging, where the best in each Group is chosen. Then those seven dogs vie for the coveted Best in Show. At the Group and Best you and your puppy how to compete successfully in the ring. These classes are usually held on a weekly basis, and you will be expected to pay a small fee to participate. Even experienced handlers may take their young puppies to such classes, just to accustom them to ring behavior and procedures. Classes like these are invaluable to you and your puppy, so be sure to take advantage if the opportunity exists.

While your dog is the one being judged according to its approximation of the breed Standard, you will find that you, his human handler, have much to do with his appearance before the eyes of the judge. Handling classes will teach you how to stack your dog, how to gait him to best advantage, how to relax in a line with other dogs, and will accustom both you and your Boxer to execute movement patterns required by the judge. If you fumble and bumble, your puppy will not look as well as he should. If you zigzag around the ring instead of going in a straight line when required, your puppy's gait may appear to be faulty even if it isn't. If you stand him in a show pose with his legs too stretched out or too close under him, his body profile may appear unattractive. In short, a successful show dog has a competent handler to present him in the best possible light to the judge. As you become more experienced, you may begin to learn some of the more advanced aspects of handling—techniques that you can use to minimize your dog's faults or make him more appealing to the judge. Handling is an art, and a very good handler can sometimes make even a mediocre dog look like a winner.

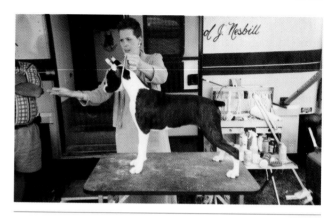

At an AKC show, a puppy's tape is always removed before entering the ring. Notice the extensive handling and grooming equipment propped against the professional handler's motor home. (S. Abraham)

SANCTIONED AND "FUN" MATCHES

Sooner or later, you will want to give your puppy some experience in competition. One of the best places to begin is at a "match" show that is either sanctioned by the American Kennel Club or sponsored by a local dog or civic organization. There are no points awarded at these events, and classes for young puppies are often a part of the program—unlike the "point" shows where 6 months is the minimum age for competition. Match shows may allow puppies as young as 8 weeks to compete. If you do take a very young pup to the match, make sure that his shots are current and do not tire him out. Personally, I like my puppy to be at least 12 weeks old before I take him to the very public venue of a dog show.

A match show is an excellent place for both you and your puppy to discover what a dog show is all about. Such shows are run with the same rules and organization as a point show, but the atmosphere is more relaxed because there are no points at stake. At most matches, no advanced entry is required, and so you can enter your puppy on the morning of the show. The majority of competitors, both puppies and humans, will be novices like you, learning to exhibit and learning the rules of competition. Even the judges may lack experience, choosing to learn to evaluate certain breeds in a relatively informal setting before they formally apply to the AKC for a license to judge a particular breed.

Matches will introduce you to other Boxer enthusiasts who may be very helpful to you—both as mentors and friends. The more experienced among them will teach you what kind of show lead and collar is best for your puppy, tell you where you can buy such equipment, advise you how to groom for the ring and critique your show ring performance if you ask them. And, of course, there will be much Boxer talk to enjoy. Remember that although it is a very human reaction to resist criticism, do not be offended if your casual "How did I do?" is met by a thoughtful evaluation that may not always include unbridled praise.

WHERE TO OBTAIN SHOW INFORMATION

Dog shows are organized by show superintendents. These professionals actually set up the physical show: the rings, the tents, designated grooming and concession areas and so on. They are also responsible for sending Premium Lists to the exhibiting public. These lists describe the individual show in great detail and contain the entry blanks needed to actually enter the show. You must enter AKC point shows in writing before the closing date designated on the entry form—usually about three weeks before the event. In order to know what shows are taking place in your area, the best reference is the "Show Events" section accompanying the *American Kennel Club Gazette*, the official publication of the AKC. You can subscribe to the *Gazette* by contacting the AKC (see appendix A). The *Gazette* also lists the names and addresses of the superintendents throughout the country. It will be helpful for you to have your name on the mailing list of the superintendents in your area; that way, you will receive Premium Lists well in advance of the shows. You can request to be on a mailing list by writing or e-mailing the superintendents of your choice. Once you actually enter dog shows, you will automatically be included on mailing lists.

The Internet is also an excellent place to obtain dog show information. Once you know the superintendents' names, you can go to their Web sites and view the dog show calendars and judging information—entire premium lists in many instances. Some Web sites are set up so that you can enter a show on-line for a small fee beyond that cited in the Premium List. This is an especially helpful service if you decide to enter a show fifteen minutes before the deadline.

ENTERING A SHOW

When faced with a Premium List for the first time, you may have questions about the requested data. It will be helpful for you to have your dog's AKC registration certificate in front of you when you begin to fill out the form. It will contain most of the information you need. You will be asked for the registered name of your dog, its sex and the AKC registration number. In addition, the breeder's name(s), the sire and dam's registered names, your dog's date of birth, country of birth and present ownership must be recorded.

You may enter in any of several classes:

- Puppy (often divided between 6-9 months and 9-12 months)

- 12– 18 months

- American Bred

- Bred by Exhibitor

- Novice

- Open (often divided between brindle and fawn)

If you are entering a puppy, it is usually most appropriate to enter him in the Puppy class.

American Bred classes are reserved for dogs bred and born in the United States. This class is most often used for dogs who are older than 18 months but not quite mature enough for Open competition.

Bred by Exhibitor means that your dog is owned or co-owned by the person or spouse of the person who was the dog's breeder. Either the breeder or a member of his immediate family may actually show the dog. Breeders are proud to show their best in this class.

Novice is a little-used class limited to dogs who have not won more than three first-place ribbons in show competition in Novice and have no more than one first prize in either Bred by Exhibitor, American Bred or Open. In addition, they must not have earned any points towards their title.

Open is often an extremely competitive class, usually filled with mature dogs. Points are statistically more often awarded to Open Class winners. However, on any given day any class winner may take the points home.

Dog show entry fees vary from show to show but are often in the $25 range as of this writing. If a Sweepstakes is offered—a competition for puppies and young dogs from 6 to 18 months, usually held at Specialty shows—an additional small fee is charged. Check the Premium List for this fee; it's usually listed in the sections devoted to trophies and prizes for a particular breed. The Sweepstakes affords no points but does award cash prizes and is a prestigious win. You enter your Sweeps class by writing in the appropriate age division and "Sweeps" in the section of the entry blank devoted to "Additional Classes." You may write one combined check for both the Sweepstakes and Regular class entry.

WHAT TO WEAR

There are no rules governing your own wardrobe at a dog show, but there are guidelines you may wish to follow. Sanctioned matches are the place for T-shirts and jeans, if that is your pleasure. Really, almost anything goes at a match, as long as it is in good taste. At point shows, on the other hand, you will see men in sport jackets, ties and casual trousers. Women usually wear suits or separates—with skirts far outnumbering pant suits. These so-called dog show dress codes are born of long tradition in the United States, harking back to an earlier era when both men and women were encouraged to think of dog shows as dress-up occasions. Whatever your choice of clothing, remember it's the dog you are showing off, not the handler! Women should remember, too, that very full skirts will undoubtedly impede the dog on the move and will not present as professional an appearance as a more conservative cut.

There is no strict dress code at a dog show, but be sure not to wear anything that will impede you or your dog's movement. (S. Abraham)

YOUR FIRST DOG SHOW

When you arrive on the show grounds, be sure to allow plenty of time to get your Boxer ready. Do not be rushed because you will communicate this to your dog, and he may not perform at his best. Be sure that your dog is clean and well groomed; for show purposes, it is customary to trim his ears and facial whiskers. It is permissible to "chalk" your dog before he is exhibited—to apply white, powdered chalk to his white areas in order to enhance his clean and sparkling appearance. But be sure to brush the chalk out before you enter the ring; it should not be flying about when the judge puts his hands on your dog! About fifteen minutes before judging begins, you should go up to the ring (listed in the Judges' Program that will be sent to you about a week before the show) and approach the steward's table. The steward is a volunteer who is present to help the judge and the exhibitors and to ensure that correct ring procedures are followed. Tell the steward what your class and number is, and he or she will give you a cardboard armband with the number printed on it. Slip the armband on (it's held in place with an elastic band), and then forget about it—but remember the number in case you are instructed by the steward to line your exhibit up in "catalog order." That way, you will know where you belong in the line.

Do not be tardy at ringside when your class is called—the judge may not wait for you. Rather, enter the ring and line up against the ringropes in a counterclockwise fashion, always mindful that your dog looks his best at all times. The judge and the steward will first check armbands for numbers, to be sure that all are present and accounted for. At that point, what happens next depends on the

The big prize! Ch. TuRo's Futurian of Cachet is shown winning Best in Show at an AKC all-breed event, handled by Gary Steele. (V & W Cook)

to move your dog so that he can view the dog in motion from different angles—some judges ask for a triangular pattern, a circle, or just "up and back." Be sure that your dog gaits in a straight line without sidewinding or crabbing.

After the judge has examined all the dogs, he will make his placements. He usually does this by pointing at his respective winners. Four ribbons are awarded per class. Hopefully, you will have occasion to proceed to the numerical markers indicating that you have placed. The judge will hand you your appropriate ribbon. You will either continue to the Winners Class because you have won a first place, or you may watch to see what happens next. If you have

preference of the individual judge. He may have the entire class circle the ring once or twice, or he may begin to evaluate each individual dog. Whatever the routine, the judge will eventually approach you.

When the judge comes to you, this is what you can expect: First, the judge will peruse your dog from a short distance away. He will then go to your Boxer's head and study it; he will open the mouth and check the bite—be prepared to open your own dog's mouth if the judge requests it. The judge will put his hands on the dog to check musculation and proper structure. If a male dog, the judge will gently check to make sure both testicles are properly descended. When he is through with his hands-on examination, the judge will ask you

Since the Boxer head, expression and bite are so prominent in the Standard, a judge will often cup the dog's head in his hands for examination. (S. Abraham)

won a second place, be sure to wait until the Winners class has been judged—you may have to reenter the ring to compete for Reserve Winners if your dog went second to the eventual point winner. Reserve Winners on rare occasions will win the points if the Winners Dog or Bitch is later declared ineligible.

After the judge awards the Winners Dog (WD) and Winners Bitch (WB) ribbons and the Reserves, the Specials class enters the ring—all the champions competing for Best of Breed honors. They are followed in line by both the Winners Dog and Winners Bitch. The judge will select his eventual Best of Breed winner from this group—and even the WD or WB is eligible for this honor. At the same time that he designates the Best of Breed, the judge will choose a Best of Opposite Sex (BOS) and a Best of Winners (BW). Best of Winners represents his choice of the better of the two point winners on that day. If more points have been awarded in one sex or another and the lesser point winner goes BW over his competition, he will obtain the maximum number of points given out on that day. In some large specialty shows, there is a Veteran's class for dogs and bitches over 6 or 7 years old. In this case, the winners of their respective Veteran's classes can also compete for Best of Breed. Sound confusing? It really isn't, and you will catch on to the rules in no time.

In especially hot weather, it is wise to carry a cooler filled with ice water and a towel so that you

You're never too old to win! Ch. Jaquet's Amaryllis is shown here winning a Veteran Bitch Class at age 9, with handler Mary Lou Hatfield. (Ashby)

can keep your dog as comfortable as possible while he is at the show. Cold water applied to the bottoms of the feet, under the neck and on the groin area does much to maintain reasonable body temperatures. A spray from a plastic water bottle is also welcomed by most dogs in torrid heat. You may also invest in a wet-down coat, which can be soaked in cold water and tied around the dog; it's usually fastened with Velcro straps. Watch carefully

While waiting her turn for examination under a tent, professional handler Erin Struff is baiting her dog to keep him interested and ready for business. (S. Abraham)

three first places in Novice. Either or both of these classes may be divided by age if specified in the Premium List for the show. The two age divisions are 10 to under 14, and 14 to 18. Age is determined as of the date of the show itself. In addition to learning to handle a dog to the highest level, Junior Showmanship competition encourages good sportsmanship and teaches many life lessons along the way. Kimberlie Steele of California won Best Junior Handler at Westminster in 1999, with the Boxer Ch. Ein-Von's Yachtsman Bay.

Twelve-year-old Danielle Butler with Ch. Minstrel's CC to Scarborough, winning the Open Junior class at the 1999 ABC Junior Showmanship Competition.

YOUR DOG'S GOOD MANNERS— AND YOURS!

As much as we love and admire our own dogs, we must remember that some Boxers are not overly fond of other Boxers. It is a fact of life that we live with—and learn to control. Therefore, remember to keep your Boxer to himself whenever you travel, and if he adopts a confrontational attitude toward any other dog, such behavior should be immediately discouraged. Often, the uniquely expressive face of the Boxer will alert his handler to a potential problem that can be solved before it escalates into an unpleasant encounter.

When long-distance travel to a dog show necessitates a stay at a motel, please be careful to walk your dog in designated areas and always bring a baggie to clean up his waste. Do not groom or bathe him in the motel room, and always make sure that dogs are permitted in whatever facility you plan to spend the night. Clean up after feeding, and do not leave your dog loose in the room, no matter how well-mannered he may be at home. A long road trip and unfamiliar surroundings may challenge the manners of any dog, and his anxiety on being separated from you may translate itself into chewing on the curtains or barking his displeasure. In addition, the housekeeping staff may enter the room and be startled by the dog—who can also use the opportunity to escape to the parking lot or the expressway nearby. A friend of mine narrowly avoided a tragedy in just this scenario: Her dog escaped through the open door of his motel room and was almost instantly struck by a car. Luckily, he recovered from his injuries. Damage to motel rooms by careless exhibitors has led to an increasingly fewer number of places that will allow dogs. We must all do what we can to remedy this sad situation.

On the show grounds themselves, proper cleanup is a must. Waste receptacles are provided

Beauty and Brains: Obedience Trials, Performance Events and Other Fun Things

The Boxer is not just another pretty face. While he can and does achieve the highest honors in conformation shows, there are many Boxers who never see the inside of a breed-conformation ring. Many of these dogs are succeeding in far-flung endeavors—Obedience, Agility, Schutzhund, Tracking, Therapy, Search and Rescue and Law Enforcement. Some of the most rewarding moments with your Boxer may come when the two of you work together to improve the quality of someone else's life, or finally get that "recall" right.

PUPPY KINDERGARTEN AND OBEDIENCE TRAINING CLUBS

You can find Obedience Training clubs through referrals from the AKC or your local kennel club. Most all-breed dog shows hold Obedience Trials as part of the day's activities, so by all means attend, learn and enjoy. Puppy Kindergarten classes are often sponsored by your local training club. Whether or not you ever enter any formal Obedience, Agility or Conformation competition, these classes may be the most important of your dog's so-called formal education. From the age of 8 weeks until 4 months, puppies of all breeds come together to learn valuable lessons in socialization. They are trained without their knowledge—all appears to be a game to them, but they are actually learning to be well-behaved canine citizens. Play days include fun with puppy-size jumps, puppy-size toys—and other puppies! Your Boxer will learn manners, leash training and "getting along with others."

When choosing to participate in the activities of an Obedience Training club in your area, be sure you are comfortable with the instructors. If they are members of the National Association of Dog Obedience Instructors (NADOI), they have passed a demanding series of conditions for membership. This does not guarantee, but does suggest, that they are competent and caring trainers who have won advanced titles with their own dogs. Beware of the

Puppy Kindergarten is essential to begin properly socializing your Boxer. (Tomita)

"overnight-wonder" trainer with little experience. Excellent trainers will be invaluable to you as you either progress beyond Kindergarten and attempt to win Trial honors, or simply desire to make your dog a more responsible canine citizen.

OBEDIENCE TRIALS AND TRIBULATIONS

Obedience Trials are held at most AKC-sanctioned shows and matches. They test the partnership of dog and handler to successfully complete a pre-scribed series of exercises. Any AKC-registered Boxer may compete in these events, and the working, athletic ability of the breed often shines through during these Obedience Trials. However, as any trainer will tell you, the Boxer is no automaton, mindlessly performing over and over again with elan. Rather, he is apt to test the ability of his trainer to hold his interest after any new exercise threatens to become boring routine.

There are three levels of Obedience expertise—Novice, Open and Utility. The Novice exercises are the simplest and really test a dog's ability to be a good companion to humans—hence the title CD for Companion Dog. In order to win the CD, your Boxer will need to achieve a score of at least 170 out of a possible 200 on three separate occasions. The highest scorers per trial will be designated as placing first through fourth, while all dogs achieving 170 or better will qualify for a "Leg," one of the three needed to achieve the Obedience title being sought.

Novice exercises involve heeling both on- and off-lead, matching the speed of the handler as it increases or decreases. Two volunteers stand facing each other so that the dog can execute a figure eight around them (on leash). He must stand

Training the Long Down in Novice Obedience. (S. Abraham)

quietly for examination, neither fearful nor hostile, while a stranger approaches and touches him. He must properly execute the Recall: While sitting at one end of the ring, he must come to his handler when called, sit squarely in front of him and then Finish by walking behind the handler to

THE AMERICAN KENNEL CLUB

Familiarly referred to as "the AKC," the American Kennel Club is a nonprofit organization devoted to the advancement of purebred dogs. The AKC maintains a registry of recognized breeds and adopts and enforces rules for dog events including shows, Obedience Trials, Field Trials, Hunting Tests, Lure Coursing, Herding, Earthdog Trials, Agility and the Canine Good Citizen program. It is a club of clubs, established in 1884 and composed today of over 500 autonomous dog clubs throughout the United States. Each club is represented by a delegate; the delegates make up the legislative body of the AKC, voting on rules and electing directors. The American Kennel Club maintains the Studbook, the record of every dog ever registered with the AKC, and publishes a variety of materials on purebred dogs, including a monthly magazine, books and numerous educational pamphlets.

Boxers waiting patiently during a Long Sit at an Obedience trial. (T. Hendrickson)

sit facing front by the handler's left side. Lastly, the dog must correctly perform the Long Sit for one minute and the Long Down for three minutes—sitting and lying in a line with other dogs, minding his own business, off lead, while his handler remains visible at the other end of the ring. The willingness with which the dog works, his attention to his handler, his correct and prompt execution of commands and a certain style all contribute to the eventual score meted out by the judge.

Open exercises are more demanding. To the basic CD requirements are added the retrieving exercises, some of which test the dog's athletic ability. No leads are used during Open. The Drop-on-Recall is added: While sitting at one end of the ring, the dog must come when called, drop (lie down) on command before he reaches his handler, return to him, sit squarely in front and Finish. Retrieving over

fences is often one of the tests that your Boxer will enjoy most. He will be required to jump over a rather high fence to retrieve a dumbbell, then return it to his handler, jumping the fence again with the object in his mouth. He must also retrieve on flat ground and execute a broad jump.

This time, the Long Sit and Long Down are extended to three and five minutes, respectively, with no handlers present or visible to the dog. The dogs are required to hold their positions even if one of their neighbors breaks and wanders over to investigate. This is a real test! Just as with the CD degree, the dogs must earn three qualifying legs in Open competition in order to receive the CDX degree—Companion Dog Excellent.

The Utility Degree is the Ph.D. of Obedience. Heeling is performed off-lead, and only hand signals are permitted. The dog must intuitively follow the pace his handler sets; no verbal commands or reprimands are allowed. In addition, Utility requires a scent-discrimination test.

Scent discrimination is fun for most Boxers. The handler will be given two objects to scent—one metal and one wood. The handler rubs his fingers on the object to transfer his scent. The judge will be given eight articles (four wood and four metal) to touch with his scent alone. The articles are all identical in appearance. The judge takes one of the handler's scented articles (using tongs or some other device that will not taint the chosen object with the judge's scent) and places it among the other eight—out of sight of dog and handler. The dog is then required to travel about 20 feet to the articles and bring back the one that is scented only by the handler. He must do a formal sit in front of the handler, followed by the usual Finish. Boxers are very good at this exercise.

The next step is a Directed Retrieve: The dog must go out and retrieve the one glove out of three that the judge selects. The gloves are placed at ring corners and the far end. The dog begins in the middle of the ring with his handler, who directs the dog to the proper glove. The dog picks up the glove and returns it to his handler. Again—only hand signals are permitted.

In the Directed-Jumping exercise, the handler instructs the dog, via hand signal or voice command, which of two jumps he should negotiate: the high jump or the bar jump. The dog starts by sitting between both jumps until he receives his command.

The last Utility exercise is a recall from the standing position. There are no long sits or stays. It is clear that there are many pitfalls that potentially face a dog going through the Utility sequence of events: He must be ever watchful and pay close attention to his handler, or else he could miss an instruction; he could pick out the wrong glove or scent article; he could miss the correct jump. Three Utility legs are required before a dog earns the Utility degree, the coveted UD.

Once the UD is achieved, the best of the Obedience titled dogs can go on to even greater glory—achieving the UDX (Utility Dog Excellent), trying to win High in Trial honors with the highest scores, or attempting to become an Obedience Trial Champion. The UDX requires the dog to already hold the UD title and receive qualifying scores in both Open and Utility at the same trial at no less than ten shows.

Still more demanding are the points that may be accumulated towards an Obedience Trial Championship (OTCh). The OTCh requires a UD title first. After that title is achieved, the dog must win 100 points and a first place in both Utility and Open, plus a third first-place win in either class, under three different judges. The Boxer will be competing against dogs of all breeds for this honor, unless he wins at a trial for Boxers only at a Specialty competition. Since a Boxer requires continual motivation for this repetitious but challenging work, an OTCh is a stunning achievement for both dog and handler. To date, only one Boxer has achieved this distinction (see p. 218), Marilyn's Tinamarie of Bropat, UDX, TD, owned by the late Steve and Marilyn Krejci. "Tina" was trained and exhibited by Marilyn.

SCHUTZHUND TRAINING

The literal English translation of the German *Schutzhund* is "protection dog." It is a challenging discipline performed outside, testing both the physical and mental capacities of the dog. It is essentially a test for working dogs, but it was developed in Germany around 1900 as a measure of which dogs would be suitable for breeding and passing along vital working ability. The emphasis at that time was on military and police work. Schutzhund trials are held at a number of locations across the United States and around the world. At present, the Boxer in Germany is second only to the German Shepherd Dog in numbers competing in Schutzhund trials annually.

The Schutzhund tests are applied to three areas: Tracking, Obedience and Protection. The Tracking phase requires the dog to find lost articles along a track that may be extremely challenging. The terrain may vary a good deal, and the dog must be extremely accurate in following the track. Often, the weather will be poor and the track may not be fresh. Dog and handler must work together closely to achieve a successful result.

The Obedience phase is in many ways similar to AKC Obedience Trials. However, the Schutzhund degree requires the dog to work in a huge field that is

Axel Von Bachbett stops the threatening "bad guy" by gripping his padded sleeve. The dog must release the grip when the man stops fighting. (G & C Markos)

many times the size of an AKC ring. The dog must work steadily while a gun is fired nearby; he must retrieve over a 3-foot jump and a 6-foot wall; he must perform a Long Down and a "Send Away."

The Protection phase is critical to Schutzhund training. It is most enlightening that the Boxer, the "family favorite" and the happy clown, succeeds in this phase of the sport when his guarding instincts are challenged. The dog must locate and hold a designated bad guy and keep him at bay; he must protect both himself and his handler from attack by an aggressive and threatening individual; and he must pass a courage test. This exercise demands total and absolute obedience to the direction of the handler and fearless courage on the part of the dog. He may have to withstand being hit twice on his side with a padded leather stick. Whenever the dog catches and stops the aggressor, he must release him immediately upon command. Dogs fail the exercise if they do not release the padded sleeve after three commands from their handler.

All of the Schutzhund tests take place on one day, and so endurance is a very important component of the successful trial dog. A point system of judging decides the trial winner for that day: 100 points is a perfect score, and 80 points are needed to pass. The dog must exhibit absolute obedience to his handler, take complex direction, exude confidence, have a willingness to defend and protect and be keen on the chase.

The Tracking phase of Schutzhund work scores both performance and concentration: 100 is a perfect score, and 70 is required to pass. This differs from AKC tracking trials, which are rated on a

Xenia Von Sparta with the 5-pound Schutzhund dumbbell required in the Schutzhund III obedience routine. (G & C Markos)

pass/fail basis. Schutzhund work requires the dog to indicate an article found at the end of a laid track by sitting, lying or standing, rather than retrieving the article itself.

Degrees are awarded at levels I, II and III, each level making greater demands on the dog. Schutzhund III is the supreme working dog. There are more and more Schutzhund enthusiasts taking up the challenge in the United States and Canada. Ivo vom Hafen, BH, SchIII, ZIP, VCCX, was bred in Germany and is owned by Cathy and George Markos from Wisconsin. Ivo, 3 years old as of this writing, is one of a very few Schutzhund III–titled dogs in the United States and was named United States Boxer Association Working Boxer of the Year in 1998. The USBA is the working Boxer club in the United States, and it sponsored three Schutzhund trials in 1998, with German judges tallying the scores. It also is a representative to the American Working Dog Federation and is the official U.S. representative to ATIBOX (Association Technique Internationale du Boxer). ATIBOX recognizes the USBA because of its commitment to preserving the working dog as well as its recognition of the FCI standard for the breed. The FCI (Federation Cynologique Internationale) began in 1911 in Europe. It includes seventy-eight member countries and recognizes 331 breeds. It is not a registry, but rather an international organization that fosters dog shows, updates and translates its own breed standards, and sponsors working, obedience and agility trials under FCI rules.

This Boxer navigates the A-frame at an Agility trial. (4U2C Photography)

AGILITY TRIALS

Agility is not really a "trial" for most Boxers. Indeed, it has been called "a controlled circus" and offers Boxers the chance to have fun and run around really fast. Nirvana for the Boxer! The fact that it requires lots of obedience training, sound athleticism and discipline, and cooperation between dog and handler is almost secondary to the joy of achievement that Agility brings.

The American Kennel Club sponsors Agility trials at many of its all-breed shows. In 1999, the American Boxer Club National Specialty included Agility on its scheduled list of events for the first time. Dogs must be at least 12 months of age to compete for titles, as the trials are physically demanding and dogs should not be tested too young. While Agility is run as a trial, to the spectator it is something of an obstacle course—the miniature golf of canine pleasure sport. Qualifying scores from the judge are required at each of three separate trials (100 is perfection, 85 is qualifying). Agility is run against the clock, and the fastest qualifiers earn the top awards on that day. Dogs must negotiate all obstacles at top speed while at the same time hitting designated "contact areas" which act as safety valves so that accuracy and safety are achieved. Different courses have different degrees of difficulty, depending on course length and the number and placement of obstacles. There are numerous award divisions, including:

- Novice Agility (NA)

- Open Agility (OA)

- Agility Excellent (AX)

- Master Agility Excellent (MX)

- Novice Jumpers with Weaves (NAJ)

- Open Jumpers with Weaves (OAJ)

- Excellent Jumpers with Weaves (AXJ)

- Champion Agility (MACH)

To achieve the MX title, a dog must earn the rank of AX and achieve qualifying scores in the AX class at ten licensed Agility trials. To achieve MACH status, he must qualify appropriately at twenty trials.

Obstacle and Jump specifications include:

A-FRAME: The dog must ascend one panel and descend the other and must touch the down panel with any part of the foot.

DOG WALK: This consists of a center plank and two ramps, one on each side of the center. The dog must ascend one ramp, cross the center plank and come down the other ramp, making contact with all three parts of the apparatus.

SEESAW: The seesaw is just that—harking back to your playground days, you will pretty well visualize it. It consists of a plank or panel balanced on a fulcrum. The dog must ascend until his weight causes the seesaw to tip and hit the ground.

PAUSE TABLE: The Pause Table is 36 inches square. The judge will require the dog to either sit or lie down on this surface for five seconds.

OPEN TUNNEL: The tunnel is a flexible tube that can be curved by the course designer. It is open on both ends and generally about 15 feet long (can be between 10 and 20 feet). The dog must enter one end and exit the other. When he begins, he cannot see the exit.

CLOSED TUNNEL: The length of the closed tunnel is 12 to 15 feet. Dogs must enter at the open end and exit through a chute.

WEAVE POLES: Weave poles consist of 6 to 12 poles that exhibit some flexibility at their base to accommodate a dog as large as a Boxer. The dog enters by passing right to left through poles 1 and 2. Then he goes left to right between poles 2 and 3, and so forth. He must properly complete the sequence of weaves or begin again until he is correct.

SINGLE-BAR JUMPS: Most Boxers are required to jump a 24-inch bar in whichever direction the judge indicates, the height of the bar being determined by the height of the dog at the withers. The Single-Bar Jump actually consists of two cross bars affixed to side stanchions. One-Bar Jumps may be added anywhere on the course, depending on its degree of difficulty.

WINDOW JUMP: This jump resembles a wall made of an opaque, clothlike material into which a 24-inch square or 24-inch-diameter circle is cut. The dog must jump through the window opening.

BROAD JUMP: This jump is usually 48 inches wide, depending on the height of the Boxer at the withers. The dog is required to jump all sections of the broad jump. He is not allowed to touch individual components of the jump.

There are other organizations sponsoring and developing Agility competitions in the United States. They include the original group that brought Agility to this country from the United Kingdom in 1986, the United States Dog Agility Association (USDAA), as well as the United Kennel Club (UKC) and the North American Dog Agility Council (NADAC). Specific rules and regulations relating to these organizations may be obtained from them directly (see appendix A for details).

In the Open Tunnel exercise, the dog cannot see the exit of the flexible tube when he enters it. (J. Brinkmann)

Jumping through the tire is exhilirating to most Agility Boxers. (K9's in Motion)

PANEL JUMPS: The panel jump appears to the dog to be a solid wall (although this is an illusion). The dog is required to jump over it without displacing it, at the direction of the judge.

THE TIRE JUMP: The dog is required to jump through a tire or other circular frame suspended in air.

The Boxer does brilliantly in Agility tests. They enable him to be an official show-off, play to the crowd and enjoy the applause. Handlers must be prepared for antics that they do not expect—all depends on the Boxer's mood of the moment!

GUIDES FOR THE BLIND

For many years, especially in the 1950s, the Boxer was one of the most popular breeds used to aid the blind. They are still used occasionally in many guide dog programs, notably the Seeing Eye program in Morristown, New Jersey. However, this facility and many others working toward the same goals have switched their preference to breeds that adapt better to kennel conditions. A number of these animals are bred by the guide dog programs themselves—notably Labrador Retrievers and Golden Retrievers. There is also a stated preference for dogs with double coats, which are more resistant to heat and cold than that of the Boxer.

Nonetheless, there are many unsighted pedestrians walking the streets of the United States and the world who are using the services of a Boxer as a guide. Breeders are justly proud that the temperament and intelligence of the breed make it so suitable for this demanding and rewarding work.

SEARCH AND RESCUE

Boxers are used with great success in times of peril and danger. During both World Wars, they were used by both sides of those conflicts as sentry and lookout dogs, pack animals, message-carriers and even herding dogs who kept cattle in check near

Boxers make reliable and effective rescue dogs. Tanis is ready for action. (R. Dyer)

the front. The Munich Boxer Club alone sent sixty dogs to help the German cause in World War I, and Philipp Stockmann, of the famous Vom Dom Kennels, accounted for ten more. Many a Boxer died in the line of duty. Today, the Boxer is occasionally in the forefront of animals called upon to search for victims of natural and man-made disasters on water and land, in the wilderness and on city streets. Notably the California Rescue Dog Association has had great success with several Boxers over the years; they have helped to locate victims of plane crashes, fire storms and earthquakes. The devastating earthquake in Turkey in August 1999 saw Boxers acting as search and "sniffer" dogs, trying to locate survivors in the rubble.

Boxers make good "sniffer" dogs. Here, Bodé searches for survivors amongst the rubble. (L & S LaValley)

Notable among canine search heroes are Jedapay's Jaunty Juba (1986–96) and Topaz Forgotten Realms "Tanis" (born in 1991), both owned by Rhonda Dyer of San Jose; Dolor's Bannor of Hearthrall (1985–93); and Trooper's Golden Echo, owned by Cindy Clark of Oak View, California. Bannor scored highest of any dog in southern California on his "mission ready" test, tracking on a ten-day-old trail and even outdoing the bloodhounds!

THERAPY WORK

There is no more rewarding aspect of Boxer ownership than the participation of the owner with his dog in bringing cheer to shut-ins, the disabled and the infirm. There are legions of stories associated with animals acting as the catalysts to dispel depression and sadness, and no breed is more suited to do this kind of work than the Boxer. His frontal eye placement and very "human" expression can often communicate effectively with the most disturbed and withdrawn among us. And the Boxer's natural *joie de vivre* is happily all too contagious in nursing and rehabilitative facilities.

There are several organizations dedicated to therapy dogs and the rights of the disabled to take them into many public places (under the auspices of the Americans With Disabilities Act 1990). Notable among these organizations are the Delta Society, established in 1977 in Portland, Oregon; Canine Companions for Independence in Santa Rosa, California; Fidos for Freedom in Laurel, Maryland; Canine Working Companions in Waterville, New York; and Paws With a Cause in Wayland, Michigan. These organizations sometimes breed their own dogs, but they often use dogs rescued from dog pounds and shelters.

Boxers work with shut-ins as Hearing Dogs, alerting people to the sound of a telephone, doorbell, smoke alarm and so on. Dogs for the Deaf, Central Point, Oregon, and Canine Hearing Companions, Vineland, New Jersey, are active Hearing Dog organizations. They act as service dogs, helping to turn on light switches and to carry and pick up items that their disabled owners

Boxers make wonderful therapy dogs. Ch. Woods End Sarmeda Legacy is a Canine Good Citizen. (K. Buckley)

LAW ENFORCEMENT

The Boxer certainly is not used in the forefront of law enforcement activity in this country. German Shepherd Dogs, by and large, take center stage in this arena. However, as Boxers have demonstrated in military and Schutzhund training, they are very well suited to protection work, and they are still occasionally used for this purpose. In addition, their keen nose and willingness to please have enabled them to become Certified Narcotics Detector Dogs, trained to find illicit drug shipments in cars, ships, airplanes and other methods of transportation. Such a dog is Dolly von den Almeauen, BH, ZTP, AD, VCCX, GCG. Dolly, now 4 years old, works as a police K-9 in a six-county area of Wisconsin, co-owned by Cathy and George Markos and her police handler Inspector Marion Byerson. Dolly is on active duty, and her work has already resulted in a felony drug charge against a suspect that Dolly identified.

CANINE GOOD CITIZENS

The American Kennel Club devised the Canine Good Citizen Test to ". . . identify and reward dogs that have the training and demeanor to be reliable family members as well as good-standing community members." A certificate from the AKC follows successful completion of the test.

Ten steps comprise the exercise, which many Boxers have passed with ease. It is open to all dogs—purebreds and mixed breeds alike. While it is not a precision drill, it does require a close

cannot manage alone. The Boxer can be taught rather easily to retrieve, though he must be encouraged to relinquish the item. The Boxer simply has to learn that playing keep-away with service items is unacceptable. Wherever there is a need, a Boxer can be trained to meet it.

working relationship between handler and dog, basic obedience and common sense. Among the steps required to pass are these:

- Accepting a Friendly Stranger (exhibiting neither aggression nor shyness on approach)

- Walking on a Loose Leash

- Walking Through a Crowd

- Sit and Down on Command (on a 20-foot lead)

- Reaction to Another Dog (demonstrating that your dog will politely tolerate another dog in his presence)

- "Supervised Separation" (a 3 minute separation from his handler, held on leash by an evaluator).

The AKC is happy to supply information and test kits for those who are interested. Your local kennel club, obedience training club or Boxer club may be involved with this stimulating and enjoyable program.

Dolly, a certified Narcotics Detector Dog, gives an "alert" by scratching the seam of a car door where drugs have been hidden. (Markos)

TEMPERAMENT TESTING

The American Temperament Test Society (ATTS), based in Fenton, Missouri, has devised an exercise not unlike the Good Citizen Test, but focusing on sound temperament rather than obedience. There are also ten required subtests, all performed on a 6-foot lead. The handler must not talk to the dog or correct or command him.

Here are a few of the subtests to give you an idea of what is entailed.

- Behavior Toward Strangers, both neutral and friendly. This evaluates the dog's sociability and protective instinct.

- Reaction to Auditory Stimuli requires the dog to respond to hidden noises and gunshots. The dog must exhibit curiosity and alertness to a rattling metal bucket and the ability to recover rapidly to abrupt noises.

- Reaction to Visual Stimulus requires the dog to react positively to a sudden visual stimulus, in this case an umbrella opened at about 5 feet from the handler and dog.

• Tactile Stimuli tests the dog's ability to negotiate unconventional footing, both plastic and wire.

• Self Protection/ Aggressive Behavior evaluates the dog's ability to recognize a nonthreatening as well as threatening situation and respond to same in a manner consistent with his breed. If he is Schutzhund trained, he is allowed to leap at the aggressive stranger, who is never closer than 10 feet from the dog.

Upon successful completion of the entire test, which takes on average

The Boxer is a versatile canine. He can be a beautiful show dog, a brilliant professional and a silly clown. (Tomita)

eight to twelve minutes, the ATTS will issue a certificate.

A DOG FOR ALL REASONS

As you can see, the Boxer is an ultimately versatile canine. He serves people in the areas of guide, therapy, search and rescue, tracking, protection and law enforcement. At the same time, he is a clown and a ham, usually a show-off at Obedience and Agility events, often to the consternation of the handler and delight of the gallery. He may elect to do a brilliant professional job on one day, and entertain the onlookers the next. Such are the joys of Boxer companionship. Most of us would not have it any other way.

Ch. Arriba's Prima Donna. (W. Gilbert)

CHAPTER 10

Headliners

I n any field, certain outstanding individuals are immediately apparent, while others are recognized only after time proves their worth. In this chapter, we honor thirteen Boxers of the past fifty years who have changed the breed in a seminal way. Some were legendary show dogs, some were extraordinary producers; in several remarkable instances, they were both. The following animals are by no means the only extraordinary Boxers that I could have chosen for discussion, but they are undeniably standouts that most admirers of the breed will honor for all time. They follow in chronological order, based on their date of birth.

CH. BANG AWAY OF SIRRAH CREST

On February 17, 1949, a flashy fawn male puppy, owned and bred by Mr. and Mrs. R. C. Harris, was whelped at their Sirrah Crest Kennels in California. He grew up to change the breed in the United States, and perhaps in all the world. He won an incredible 121 all-breed Best in Shows in his five-year career, handled by Nate Levine, including BIS at Westminster in 1951. When you consider that there were far fewer dog shows in those days, it makes his achievements all the more impressive. However, he made his greatest contribution as the Legion of Merit Sire of eighty-one U.S. champions (including seven Producers), a record that still stands today. A dominant sire, bred to approximately 200 bitches in his lifetime, Bang Away's descendants made a tremendous impact on the show and breeding world. Higher stationed than the Boxers of the 1930s and '40s, they went on to reproduce, in turn, the many virtues for which their sire was famous.

A product of intense line breeding on Utz and Dorian descendants, Bang Away's dam, Verily Verily, was very strong in head and eye, with great vitality and élan. Ursa Major had the great running gear and was tall, rather reserved and quite elegant. Bang Away combined the best of both, representing only the fourth generation of Sirrah Crest breeding. His five-generation pedigree is worth studying—it includes only thirty individual dogs out of a theoretical sixty-two possibilities.

Bang Away had showmanship that made him stand out as a "great one." Mrs. Phoebe Harris, his owner, said he always seemed to be looking for something just beyond the horizon—tail up, muscles taut, in perfect show stance. He not only passed along this vibrant attitude toward life, but also his flashy good looks, clean-limbed lines and more elegance than the breed was accustomed to seeing at that time. He was a flashily marked dog, and his eye-catching appearance made such a lasting impression on the fancy that from that time forward "flash" became a prized attribute. When he

Ch. Bang Away of Sirrah Crest, Legion of Merit Sire. [Ch. Ursa Major of Sirrah Crest x Verily Verily of Sirrah Crest.] (collection of E. Linderholm Wood)

was only 13 weeks old, Bang Away was judged by Frau Stockmann at a specialty puppy match in California. She declared that he would be "the greatest dog in America." She published his photo in the German *Boxer Blatter* with the caption "Little Lustig." Some months later, he went on to win BOW at the American Boxer Club Specialty, from the 9–12-month Puppy Class.

Bang Away's fame transcended the show ring. He was featured in the popular magazines of the day, such as *Colliers, Life* and *Time.* People who knew nothing of show dogs knew Bang Away. Airline pilots were proud to fly him to his many show destinations, and he rode serenely in the cabin on many occasions. He did so much to popularize the breed, the Boxer enjoyed a sharp increase in registrations during his time in the limelight. (See chapter 2.)

His show career was indeed the stuff of legends, and in 1956 a testimonial retirement dinner was held for him by the American Boxer Club at the Savoy-Plaza Hotel in New York City. Bang Away sat right at the table with a gold crown on his head and ate steak fed to him piece by piece on a fork. As the plaque presented to him by the ABC concludes, "To all of us, Bang Away himself

*Ch. Jered's Spellbinder, Sire of Merit.
[Ch. Elixir of Raineylane x Hot Copy of
Gay Oaks.]*

*Bang Away's first point show, winning the 9–12-month Puppy Class at the
1950 American Boxer Club Specialty. (collection of E. Linderholm Wood)*

remains every inch a king and an inspiration to be carried forever in our hearts."

CH. JERED'S SPELLBINDER

Bred and owned by Mr. and Mrs. Edward Garich, Spellbinder was whelped in 1951. His sire, Elixir, was a son of Mazelaine's Kapellmeister (thirty-four champions). Kapellmeister's sire, Merry Monarch, was by a Dorian son out of an Utz daughter. Spellbinder's dam was a linebred product of Sirrah Crest bloodlines, heavy in crosses to Utz and Dorian. Spellbinder sired fifty-six champions during a time when Bang Away was attracting the great majority of consorts. Among his get were Ch. Dempsey's Copper Gentleman and Ch. Treceder's Selection. Selection went on to sire sixteen champions, including the two great producers Ch. Treceder's Shine Boy and Ch. Treceder's Sequel. Spellbinder, through his son Wardrobe's Delharts Mack the Knife, is also the great grandsire of Pat Heath's great English champion Seefeld Picasso. It is interesting to note that Spellbinder is the only headliner who does not trace back to Bang Away.

CH. BARRAGE OF QUALITY HILL

Barrage was Bang Away's top-producing son, whelped in l953 and bred by Mr. and Mrs. M. E. Grenier, Jr. Barrage was campaigned initially by

Ch. Barrage of Quality Hill, Legion of Merit Sire. [Ch. Bang Away of Sirrah Crest x Valley Grove's Applause.]

handler Larry Downey for his breeders, then extensively by Jane Forsyth when he was sold to Mr. and Mrs. Jouett Shouse. Mr. Shouse was Assistant Secretary of the Treasury and Chairman of the Democratic National Committee in a long and distinguished career as a statesman. As a show dog, Barrage won the Group at Westminster in 1957 and caused a great sensation when he topped his famous sire in 1955 for Best American Bred in Show (when Bang Away was 6 years old). Barrage won Best of Breed at the ABC specialty in 1955 (from the Classes) and 1957, losing in 1956 to his littermate, the bitch Ch. Baroque of Quality Hill.

However, as brilliant a record as he had in the ring, winning many Groups and Best in Shows, it was as a producer that he left his greatest mark on the breed.

Barrage gave us seven Producers among his forty-five champions. Among his famous offspring were Ch. Salgray's Battle Chief and Ch. Marquam Hill's Flamingo (sire and dam of the famous "F" litter and of great importance in the foundation of Salgray Boxers), as well as the fine winners Ch. Eldic's Darius (sire of thirteen champions), Ch. Cajon's Calling Card (twenty-five champions) and Ch. Terudon's Kiss Me Kate. It was to Barrage that Dr. and Mrs. Lloyd Flint bred their two foundation bitches, both sired by the Bang Away son Ch. Steeplechase Up and Away. These breedings established the important Flintwood line. Barrage was tall and smooth, very much in the tradition of his sire. He, too, was featured in the magazine art of the day, and he was cover dog for the February 1957 issue of *Sports Illustrated*. He left an indelible imprint on the breed.

CH. SALGRAY'S FLYING HIGH AND CH. SALGRAY'S FASHION PLATE

Flying High and Fashion Plate were two of America's most important sires. Littermates born in 1961, and bred by Daniel and Phyllis Hamilburg of Salgray Boxer fame, they were a product of a half-sister to a half-brother mating, as both their sire and dam were by Barrage. Flying High is a Legion of Merit Sire with twenty-seven champions; Fashion Plate left behind sixty-three champion

Ch. Salgray's Flying High, Legion of Merit Sire. [Ch. Salgray's Battle Chief x Ch. Marquam Hill's Flamingo.]

Massachusetts. Flamingo had been purchased as a youngster after Phyllis saw her at Jane Kamp Forsyth's Grayarlin Kennels, and Salgray's own Battle Chief was their first homebred champion. In addition to the two famous "F" brothers, that first Battle Chief to Flamingo breeding included four additional bitch champions, Flamecrest, Frolic, Fanfare and Flaming Ember, making a total of six champions in one litter. When Flaming Ember was bred back to her litter brother Flying High, in a daring and brilliantly successful experiment in inbreeding, she gave the fancy Ch. Salgray's Ambush (a Legion of Merit Sire of seven Producers) and the beautiful Ch. Salgray's Auntie Mame, dam of three champions in her own right. A second breeding of Battle Chief to Flamingo produced Ch. Salgray's Memory Book, dam of three champions including the Best in Show winning Ch. Salgray's Jitterbug.

The Hamilburgs inbred and linebred carefully and with great attention to plan. Their intent was to establish a "type" with which they would carry on through the years—and so they did. The "typical" Salgray Boxer was a long-legged, beautifully balanced animal with an elegant arch of neck and a clean, correct head that was more "bricklike" than square. Fashion Plate and Flying High reproduced this type more often than not, no matter what bitches were brought to them. Their dominance helped to continue the Boxer's gradual transition from the shorter-legged and less stylish animals that had gone before. What Bang Away and Barrage began, the "F" brothers, descendants of both of these famous forbears, reinforced.

sons and daughters. Both brothers were multiple Best in Show winners, and Fashion Plate was the ABC Best of Breed in 1965 and 1966.

These two animals represented only the second generation of Salgray breeding at their kennel in

Ch. Holly Lane's Windstorm, Legion of Merit Dam. [Ch. Brayshaw's Masquerader x Ch. Holly Lane's Cookie.]

CH. HOLLY LANE'S WINDSTORM

The beautiful Group-winning Windstorm, one of the few "ladies" to win Legion of Merit honors (along with Moon Valley's Merry Weather and Merrilane's Mad Passion, CD), was whelped in 1966. Her dam, Cookie, was a Ch. Flintwood Sundowner daughter and represented the first generation of breeding for Dr. and Mrs. E. A. McClintock of Kansas. Windstorm's sire, Masquerader, was a double Bang Away grandson. Bred four times, she produced a total of eleven champions, eight of them in just two litters by Ch. Scher-Khoun's Meshack. Of her many titled offspring, three sired by Meshack went on to be ABC Sires and Dams of Merit: Ch. Holly Lane's Winter Storm, Ch. Holly Lane's Deliteful Replay and Ch. Holly Lane's Diamond Replay. Windstorm is actually tied with Gretel v. Hohenneuffen as the record holder producing the most U.S. champions, but Gretel was German-bred and was imported to the United States in whelp for her first litter here in the 1930s.

Windstorm, heavy in Barrage and Bang Away bloodlines, proved to be a dominant bitch whether linebred (as in her litters by Ch. Holly Lane's Disk Wheel and Ch. Holly Lane's Night Wind) or relatively outcrossed. She stamped her offspring with her indelible type, beautiful topline and sound temperament.

CH. MILLAN'S FASHION HINT

Fashion Hint's dam was a Flying High daughter. Therefore, he was strongly linebred to the Salgray Boxers. Born in 1966, and bred and owned by

Michael Millan of Canada, Fashion Hint's record as a sire is unparalleled. Among his sixty-six champions, there were no less than twelve Producers—a stunning achievement that not even the great Bang Away equaled.

In 1981, seven years after Fashion Hint's death, Dr. Lloyd Flint of Flintwood Boxers wrote, "Fashion Hint was proven to be the most prepotent sire of the past twenty-five years for the qualities set forth in the Standard. It is still unusual for so many genes to have doubled up in one animal as to have stamped his offspring to the extent that they are unmistakable in the show ring through several generations." Fashion Hint was consistent in reproducing fine chiseled heads, excellent balance and angulation, good shoulders and an ideal combination of style with elegance.

His career as a stud dog overlapped that of his famous sire and grandsire, and breeders of the time had a chance to use all three dogs. It was truly a glorious time for the American Boxer breeder. To add to the mix, Fashion Hint's very first litter produced a dog who actually rivaled his own prepotency, Ch. Scher-Khoun's Shadrack of Ben and Shirley De Boer's Scher-Khoun Kennels outside

Ch. Millan's Fashion Hint, Legion of Merit Sire. [Ch. Salgray's Fashion Plate x Am. Can. Ch. Gaymitz Jet Action.]

Toronto. Shadrack himself accounted for no less than forty-two champions and nine Producers. Fashion Hint's twelve Producers of Merit include Ch. Merrilane's Holiday Fashion, Ch. Salgray's Jitterbug, Ch. Von Schorer's Moonshadow, Ch. TuRo's Native Dancer, Ch. Becrelen's Import, Ch. Aracrest's Amnesty—all very influential and important to the future of the kennels they represented and those who bred to them or bred their offspring.

CH. ARRIBA'S PRIMA DONNA

"Suzie," as she was affectionately known, was arguably one of the top show dogs of either sex that the breed has seen before or since. As her owner, Dr. Theodore Fickes of Arriba Boxers said, "She never had a bad day." This attitude translated itself into a presence in the ring that transcended whatever faults she may have had—much as had been the case with her ancestor Bang Away so many years before.

Whelped in 1966, Prima Donna came to Ted Fickes almost as if the Fates decreed it. Here's the story: A gentleman named Virgil Baribeault had approached Ted to see if he had any flashy fawn males for sale as pets. As it happened, he did not. Mr. Baribeault decided to purchase Arriba's Alicia instead, in order to breed his own fawn male. When Alicia eventually came into season, Mr. Baribeault put himself in Ted's capable hands to plan the breeding. Alicia was from a litter by Ch. Mazelaine's Early Times x Nahum's Arriba ("Reba")—a Ch. Eu-Bet's Typecutter daughter. Reba was unique in that nowhere did she cross back to Bang Away or Barrage, so Ted decided to mate Alicia to Dr. Flint's Ch. Flintwood's Live Ammo, himself a product of a very scientific crossing and recrossing of animals that were linebred on Barrage. When Alicia's litter was born, there was Mr. Baribeault's flashy fawn dog! He was so delighted that he offered Ted the remaining two bitches for the equivalent of $62.50 apiece. And so Prima Donna came to reside at Arriba Kennels.

"Suzie" was Best of Breed at ABC in 1969, taking revenge for her BOS (to Ambush) the year before. In only eighteen months of campaigning by Jane Forsyth (while co-owned with Dr. and Mrs. P. J. Pagano), Suzie amassed twenty-three Best in Shows, culminating with her stunning Best in Show at Westminster in 1970, and she was the only Boxer bitch before or since to achieve this distinction. Her record for most Best in Shows in the shortest time span has yet to be eclipsed by any bitch. *Kennel Review Magazine* designated her one of the Top Ten Working Dogs of all time. In only his sixth year after beginning the Arriba line, and while still in his 20s, Dr. Fickes had a once-in-a-lifetime show dog.

Suzie was less successful in the whelping box than the show ring. She produced only two potential show puppies, and they did not live up to their mother's reputation. However, Suzie's bitch pup by Fashion Hint, Arriba's Maggie Mae, was sold to Argentina and became the dam of the leading sire in South America. Suzie lived nearly fourteen happy years.

CH. SCHER-KHOUN'S SHADRACK

Shadrack, from Fashion Hint's very first litter at just over a year of age, was bred and owned by Ben and Shirley De Boer of Toronto. Whelped in 1967, Shadrack sired forty-two champions and no less than nine Producers. His dam, Carousel, was by Can. Ch. Standfast of Blossomlea out of a Standfast daughter. As Standfast was himself a Spellbinder grandson on his dam's side, Shadrack brings together the great producing lines of Bang Away/Barrage and Spellbinder. His influence was far-reaching, and Shadrack sons and daughters became the mainstays for many kennels that were starting out at the time. Among these were Donessle, who bred the Shadrack daughter Can. Ch. Donessle's Miss Fancy to LOM Sire Ch. Gray Roy's Minstrel Boy and produced five American champions, one Sire of Merit and one Canadian Dam of Merit; Scarborough, whose Ch. Scher-Khoun's Tarantella's first litter by Minstrel Boy included the DOM and SOM Scarborough Soliloquy and Ch. Scarborough Silversmith; Omega Boxers, who finished the plain fawn dog Omega's Rockfire and linebred intensively through

Ch. Scher-Khoun's Shadrack, Legion of Merit Sire. [Ch. Millan's Fashion Hint x Can. Ch. Scher-Khoun's Carousel.]

his son Ch. Aracrest's Talisman; and Mephisto Boxers, whose foundation bitch, Ch. Scher-Khoun's Autumn Concerto was a result of Shadrack bred back to his grand-dam, Apricot Brandy. The De Boer's own Ch. Scher-Khoun's Meshack, a product of Shadrack inbred to his litter sister Syncopation, became a leading sire himself who was especially known for his winning and producing get out of the great Windstorm.

Breeder/owner handled by Ben and Shirley, Shadrack was a great winner in his own right, on both sides of the border, topping the breed at ABC in 1972. He was a Best in Show winner and one of the top dogs in Canada, all-breeds. His bloodline is still prized today, almost twenty-five years after his death.

CH. MARQUAM HILL'S TRAPER OF TURO

"Traper," sire of sixty-seven champions, holds top honors for the most champions sired by a single dog after Bang Away. He is a close second to Fashion Hint for the most Producers sired of all time (ten). His Canadian-bred sire Vendetta is a Shadrack grandson, and his dam is by Ch. Benjoman of 5Ts, a Shadrack grandson. While certainly not an inbred animal, Traper was loosely linebred on Fashion Hint to hopefully assure his prepotency and dominance.

Bred by Dr. Robert Burke of Marquam Hills Kennels in 1980, Traper arrived at 8 weeks old at the TuRo Kennels of Elizabeth Esacove and Sandy Roberts of Houston. His litter brother, the fawn Ch. Marquam Hill's Trigger of TuRo, was also a Sire of Merit. Traper was a bold, striking dog with lots of bone and substance. He took a long time to mature. He was a perfectly balanced 25½ inches, with expressive eyes and an especially wide under-jaw—all characteristics that he was able to pass along with great consistency. Most of all, Sandy Roberts remembers "More than anybody we ever owned, he was huggy and people-oriented." His especially sweet disposition showed up again and again in his offspring.

Several of Traper's get have played pivotal roles in the Boxer world. Ch. Wagner Wilvirday Famous Amos was Best of Breed at ABC for an

Ch. Marquam Hill's Traper of TuRo, Legion of Merit Sire. [Ch. Mephisto's Vendetta x Ch. TuRo's Whisper of 5Ts.]

unprecedented four wins—and accounted for sixteen Groups and four all-breed Best in Shows. He is a Sire of Merit. Traper's daughter Ch. TuRo's Cachet was twice a Westminster Group winner (see below). When bred to TuRo's Touche, DOM, a Benjoman of 5Ts daughter, he produced three very influential males: Ch. TuRo's Empire, SOM, sired Ch. Treceder's All That Jazz, #1 Boxer in 1989 and 1990; TuRo's Emblem went to Japan and became a primary influence in that country; and TuRo's Escappade became a Sire of Merit and gave us the great bitch Ch. Kiebla's Tradition of TuRo (see below). Ch. Golden Haze Tuxedo, a Legion of Merit sire, is a Traper son whose influence will be far-reaching. His own son, Ch. Josha's Linebacker, SOM, was one of the most sought-after sires of the 1990s. Today, breeders across the nation continue to build on the Traper legacy.

CH. TuRo's CACHET

Ch. TuRo's Cachet (Ch. Marquam Hill's Traper of TuRo x TuRo's Katerina of Cross Bar): Never was a youngster welcomed with more high expectations than the bitch TuRo's Cachet, a birthday present from Len Magowitz's wife, Susan. Whelped in January 1982, bred by TuRo, Cachet became the foundation bitch for, fittingly, Cachet Boxers of New York. Her dam, Katerina, DOM, was by the very influential double Fashion Hint son, Ch. TuRo's Native Dancer (eighteen champions). Therefore, when bred to Traper, Cachet produced puppies that were linebred to Fashion Hint, albeit somewhat distant on the sire's side.

Cachet never disappointed. When her show career ended in 1987, she had accounted for 33 Best in Shows, 137 Group Firsts and 40 Specialties. She was Best of Breed at ABC in 1986. Her back-to-back Working Group wins at Westminster in 1986 and 1987 were remarkable achievements. She was handled throughout her career by Chic Ceccarini and later his granddaughter, Kim Pastella. Not content with just her show laurels, Cachet was an important producer as well.

Cachet's litter by Ch. TuRo's Empire produced the champions Cachet's Mad Max of TuRo, SOM, and Cachet's Casablanca of TuRo. Casablanca is the grandsire of Ch. TuRo's Futurian of Cachet, an ABC Best of Breed and Westminster Group winner in 1996.

Not an extremely tall or rangy bitch, Cachet was of perfectly square proportions—all parts in moderation. Her head was typical and lovely, and for many people she represents the epitome of Boxer breed type in the female. She was a happy dog in the ring, though not a dynamic showman—making her magnificent success in the ring all the more remarkable. Throughout her long life, she continued to attract attention and admiration from the fancy.

CH. KIEBLA'S TRADITION OF TuRo

The irrepressible "Tiggin" was bred by Kitti Barker and co-owned by Kitti Barker, Bruce and Jeanne Korson and Sandy Roberts. Her sire, Escappade, was a Traper son from his highly successful cross

(Tomita)

CHAPTER 11

Matchmaking: Should You Breed Your Boxer?

At one time or another, almost all of us have contemplated a delicious prospect: a whelping box filled with healthy, beautiful puppies and doting moms—both the canine and human variety—keeping affectionate watch over the babes. Nice scenario, but the truth is that unless you purchased your Boxer dog or bitch specifically as a breeding prospect from a very reputable breeder, overseeing the planning, whelping and raising of healthy and well-socialized puppies is beyond the capability of most loving owners. It's very hard work, monumentally time-consuming and often frustrating in the extreme.

STATISTICS AND CANINE OVERPOPULATION

In the twelve calendar months of 1999, the Boxer ranked tenth among all breeds according to the numbers registered with the AKC. Almost 35,000 Boxers, most of them puppies, joined the ranks of purebred dogs. To most breeders, these are frightening numbers. Does the American public have enough responsible dog owners to assimilate such large numbers, and might even more popularity put the breed at great database of acceptable ratings is limited. However, it is sure to become more popular because of the early diagnosis it affords. PennHIP also evaluates osteoarthritis as a part of the rating confirming or denying hip dysplasia in your Boxer.

Cardiac Abnormalities

You should have your Boxer evaluated for both subaortic stenosis (SAS) and cardiomyopathy. While SAS can be ruled out at a relatively young age (by means of an echo Doppler to determine blood velocity in the aorta), the tests for cardiomyopathy are much more problematic—at present an EKG, echocardiogram and Holter monitor. The best that these tests can do is rule out the presence of disease at the time the tests are taken, but many a Boxer may develop the condition as he or she ages. Nonetheless, the first essential line of defense is to perform these tests. If your Boxer exhibits significant abnormalities, he or she clearly should not be bred. The American Boxer Club is funding research into finding genetic markers for BCM (Boxer Cardiomyopathy), as well as establishing test parameters and guidelines.

Thyroid

Low levels of thyroid hormones may predispose your Boxer to infertility among many other ills. It is prudent to check the thyroid levels of breeding animals to make sure that all is well (see chapter 6). If the test reveals that your Boxer has an insufficient amount of circulating thyroid hormone, you can provide a supplement in the form of oral medication. It would be wise to do some real soul-searching before you breed a Boxer who would be infertile without the use of oral thyroid supplementation.

So You Want to Be a Breeder?

In October 1972, while my husband was away at a dog show, I stayed home to whelp our very first litter. After careful planning and much anticipation, we had bred our beautiful champion bitch to a fine dog, an arrangement endorsed by "Heidi's" highly successful breeder and our mentor. The whelping proceeded smoothly. When it was over, we had four white puppies, assorted so-called plain ones and three flashy pups who were the designated show prospects. In the ensuing weeks, we endured toxic milk, mastitis, septicemia and the deaths of several in the litter despite our best efforts. Of the three show prospects, we ended up with a bitch who showed her lower incisors at maturity, a monorchid dog (dog with only one testicle) and another who was unfortunately placed in a dysfunctional home where he was loved but never shown. It was not an auspicious beginning.

Disappointments in the whelping box, even small tragedies, happen to all breeders with any experience. The gentle art of breeding dogs offers no guarantees for success. If everything can and often does go wrong with even the best-laid plans, it is therefore all the more imperative to make decisions wisely and well, before the would-be brood bitch meets her consort. Long in advance of the first signs of a bitch's season, her owners, who are after all the official breeders of the litter, should have

The sire of this award-winning litter is brindle, while the dam is fawn. L–R: Ch. Trefoil's Fiddlesticks; Trefoil's Frequent Flyer; Trefoil's Flamestitch; Ch. Trefoil's Finesse; Trefoil's Flashpoint, DOM. (M. Adams)

developed a strategy to minimize the variables and encourage the odds of producing that nearly perfect puppy. In addition to more subjective assessments, the bitch should be current on all inoculations and free of parasites. If she is on a systemic flea-control method such as Frontline or Bio Spot, these preparations should probably be discontinued before breeding. Likewise, any heartworm preventive must be evaluated for its potential effect on conception or developing embryos. Conventional veterinary wisdom indicates "no problems," but the skeptics among us still wonder.

When I interviewed several breeders to determine what they thought were the most important considerations in dog breeding, they told me many things, including "I have a flaw in my character that makes me want to go into endless debt," and "I keep my fingers crossed and I pray." But in each interview I learned that all of us who really care about what we are producing have reasons that are, for us, very critical. One breeder stated that she did a particular breeding because she wanted to preserve a rare old bloodline. Another told me that she used a certain stud dog because he was known to produce excellent bitches and that's what she wanted to keep in the litter; she didn't care if the dogs were only mediocre. No one said they wanted to make a profit, but we would be naive to think that such motivation does not exist. While our reasons for doing what we do are as variable as the people in the sport, a few imperatives are clear.

Breeding your Boxer can be rewarding, but there may be many pitfalls along the way to an outstanding litter. (M. Adams)

First, you must take a long, critical look at your prospective dam. Even though she may be a champion, she might just be the benefactress of some bad judging. And even if she is stunning, champion or not, she still has faults. All dogs have faults. Hopefully, you will know what they are, though you may not admit to them very often. If you aren't sure what the faults may be, seek some trusted and experienced advice. If you are a novice and three successful breeders tell you your bitch should not be bred at all, acknowledge that they may be right.

STUDY YOUR BREED STANDARD

As discussed in chapter 3, the breed Standard is the description of the ideal Boxer, and as a breeder you should be striving to produce it. If your pride and joy is a worthwhile representative of the Boxer breed, you should start to review show catalogs, Boxer magazines and studbooks to aid in your search for the ideal mate. Sperm is easy to find, but the perfect choice of stud dog is not an easy or casual decision. Some breeders only want to breed to the top winner of the day. This can be a wonderful idea or a perfect disaster. The greatest ring hero, the one who garners all the oohs and aahs, may not be genetically suitable for your female. He may only "nick" with (in breeder's terminology, means "click" with) certain bloodlines—or none at all. None of us can be quite sure why certain stud dogs and brood bitches are dominant for a variety of desirable traits, while their littermates produce straight shoulders and light eyes. I consider it one of Nature's tantalizing mysteries. A dominant producer is a treasure beyond price to the true breeder. Years ago, I bred to such an animal because I wanted the clean, leggy look he was siring. I still see his influence almost twenty-five years later.

Linebreeding, Inbreeding and Outcrossing

Many believe that linebreeding is the only way to go. This involves the practice of breeding not-so-close relatives in hopes of perpetuating and intensifying the "good" genes. Likewise, inbreeding—breeding close relations such as full brother to full sister or father to daughter—is favored by some. I don't believe that there is any one right choice to be made in this regard. Rather, you have to know your gene pool; that is, you have to know whether or not you are likely to foster good or bad traits by concentrating genetic material in this way. Some Boxers will benefit from this practice; others will not be so fortunate. Proceed with caution! Remember that the Boxer gene pool is not very large in this country. All the Boxers in the United States, with very few exceptions, came from one or another of the four German foundation sires and also have Bang Away in their pedigrees. These five dogs are responsible for almost all the Boxers alive in the States today. Their genes, dominant or recessive, whether fostering illness or good health, good temperaments or bad and excellent conformation or not, must be studied carefully before they are concentrated in a program of intense linebreeding or inbreeding with the descendants of these dogs.

My most gratifying successes as a breeder have come from outcrossing—breeding individuals who are not very closely related. As noted above, they *are* likely to be related a few generations back since Bang Away and the German imports appear in almost every pedigree if you trace back far enough in the United States. However, if you look at just three or four generations of my pedigrees, the same names seldom appear twice. That works for me, but it won't work for everyone. I think that the study of pedigrees, while invaluable for many reasons, is sometimes misleading, especially to the novice. Many times I've heard excited friends anticipating that great litter because "it looks fabulous on paper" or because "there are thirty champions in four generations." Paper dogs are, unfortunately, only paper dogs. Some of the world's worst animals have some of the most impressive pedigrees. When I contemplate a breeding, pedigree does play a part, sometimes an important one, but rarely is my goal to concentrate a bloodline.

My immediate intention is usually fault-offset breeding—countering the faults of one parent with the virtues of the other. To me, the phenotype (what the dog looks like) is more important than the genotype (the makeup of his genetic material). Of course, if I have a bitch with a questionable topline, I will not elect to breed her to a stud dog who shares this fault or tends to produce it. So to a degree I *am* watching the pedigree. But if a dog's production record is variable or unknown, I pay far greater attention to what he *looks* like. I would not want to breed two significant faults together. Neither would I be likely to go to the other extreme and breed, for example, a bitch short on leg to a gazelle-like dog. I actually have done those things before and most often these matings have resulted in either gazelles or toads, rarely the hypothetical blend I had imagined. Now, though, I would choose to breed to *type*, to go to a correct dog who was, on balance,

When contemplating a breeding, you must study your dog's bloodlines in order to make the best pairing. (M. Adams)

strong in the characteristics lacking in my bitch. With this philosophy in mind, we repeated a particular mating three times and produced five champions, including Group and Specialty winners, as well as an ABC Sire of Merit.

Knowledge really is power when it comes to breeding. Find out about the bitch's past breeding history, if any. Did she whelp easily? Did she need a C-section due to uterine inertia, a rather common complaint among some bitches? If she had a terrible time with her last litter, if she had supperative mastitis, if she had eclampsia, if you were afraid you might even lose her, do you think it would be wise to tempt fate a second time? No wall of purple ribbons is worth the prospect of an early death.

WHAT ABOUT TEMPERAMENT?

Even the most beautiful bitch or dog in the world from the healthiest of breeding stock may prove to be a terrible disappointment if she or he cringes every time the wind rustles the leaves in the trees.

Unstable temperament is, unfortunately, one of the easiest qualities to perpetuate in the Boxer—much easier than strong bites or good pasterns. Only you, the breeder, really know whether or not your Boxer turns to mush at a moment's notice, shies at strangers or acts aggressively out of fear. Remember, too, that a falling chair or a lunge from a passing dog at a show is no excuse for a lifetime of cringing or cowardice. How many excuses will you make for this insecure animal? Sound-tempered dogs take setbacks in their stride. Not only the brood bitch, but also the stud dog must be of an absolutely sound mind. No dog should be offered at public stud unless he has a bold, outgoing attitude toward life, exemplifying the best personality traits of the Boxer.

ASSESSING YOUR GOALS

After you have painstakingly evaluated your bitch, determined her faults and virtues and satisfied yourself that she is healthy and of stable disposition, you might want to sit down and decide what you want from the upcoming litter. Can you honestly say that you are seeking to improve the breed? Do you have legitimate dreams of a great show winner, and are you prepared to raise and train and nurture for many years to come? Are you confident that you can place the pet-quality puppies in loving and responsible homes? Can you afford the $400 to $800 fee that is a common figure to pay to the owner of the dog for stud service? Can you afford to pay for a C-section if necessary, or the expensive milk replacement should the bitch prove empty?

Take your Boxer's temperament into account before breeding. These two puppies grew up to be champions. (J & L Huffman)

Are you aware that some veterinarians charge a considerable fee to crop ears? Or do you really just want to sell pups to pay your taxes or help with the down payment on a condo? There is a very big difference between a respected breeder and a person who just wants to sell puppies.

REVERE YOUR GOOD ADVISORS

You probably have very few mentors—people who are able to assess your problems and aspirations with objectivity, advisors who care. Beware

the folk who turn every discussion around to
extol the merits of their stud dog or try to sell
you a puppy every time they see you. Get to
know the most admired people in the Boxer
world and heed their words of wisdom. These are
the people who said to me long ago that I might
consider breeding to the sire of a striking youngster, not the youngster himself, because the older
dog's record as a producer was sterling and the
son was untried. These are the people who told
me not to worry about superstitions that one
should never repeat a successful breeding. These
are the people you can call at 3 A.M. for advice
because you have a dying puppy. These are the
people who are truly committed to the Boxer
because they really love the breed and what is
best for it—and you.

"BREEDER" DEFINED

If it was easy to breed outstanding specimens, there
would probably be more people doing it. We are all
aware of the many who leave the sport because of
bad advice, bad luck or bad karma. Conventional
wisdom says that most breeders are "in and out of
dogs" within five years. Nature offers no guarantees.
The stayers, the ones with the brilliant success stories, have learned to be geneticists and psychologists
and anatomy experts. They have elected to perse-
vere in spite of failure and heartbreak. They have
established a peerless record of producing happy
and stable winners over many years, ever mindful
that the show dog is also a beloved pet. They give
advice willingly. They define the word *breeder*.

STUD DOG MANAGEMENT

A male Boxer offered at stud must pass all the
clearances and fulfill all the same temperament
requirements as his female consort. In addition,
the bitch should be required to furnish to the stud
dog owner a certificate that she has been tested
free of canine brucellosis, a bacterial infection that
can be transmitted by sexual contact, ingestion of
contaminated organic materials or even congeni-
tally from one or both parents. While not common, it is very serious, and both dog and bitch
should be tested clear. A simple blood test is all
that is necessary. It is customary for the bitch to
visit the male for the actual service, accompanied
by the owner or shipped by air if the distance is
considerable. In the 1990s, the pioneering efforts
of using chilled and frozen semen enabled many a
good male to perpetuate his genes with a minimum of effort, and in some cases even after his
death. Statistically, more puppies are born from
natural breedings, but advances in insemination
techniques (such as intracervical insemination) are
making the use of fresh and chilled semen more
reliable all the time.

It is common for two breedings to be offered,
usually forty-eight hours apart. Timing is everything, and blood tests on the bitch to determine
progesterone levels and the time of ovulation are
becoming increasingly more useful in the canine
reproduction field. Several of these tests at any one
estrus cycle may be required, and the bitch owner
should be aware that they can involve significant
expense. The most potent stud in the world cannot

A dominant sire like Ch. Bridgewood's B.K. Kahuna can stamp his look on his progeny, even when bred to bitches of different bloodlines. (M. Adams)

make babes if the sperm have deteriorated by the time the bitch is actually ready for her eggs to be fertilized.

As the owner of the stud dog, you have two primary responsibilities. You must ensure that loving homes are found for any pups your dog sires, and you must provide proper facilities to keep the visiting bitch in your home or kennel. Remember that some bitches are consummate escape artists! Years ago, a canine visitor to our home, left in her crate in our closed kitchen, broke free of the crate and went through a window screen while we were absent. Luckily, we timed our arrival with her leap to freedom and all was well—but it was a lesson learned.

Lastly—remember that your male Boxer will be the same loving dog after a breeding as he was before a breeding. Stud work may make him less tolerant of other males, but it will not affect his basic sweet disposition with his people.

CUTTING THE DEAL

Any arrangements between stud dog owner and brood bitch owner should be in writing and well understood by all parties involved before the breeding takes place. Payment is usually the first point of negotiation. Sometimes the stud dog owner will be willing to breed for no fee in exchange for his choice of a puppy. Be sure to determine in advance what choice of puppy he will get—first (pick of the litter) or second (after your choice), for example. There will have to be arrangements in the case that there is only one puppy in the litter, or if the markings of the puppies are

unacceptable for any reason. When a fee is involved, it is customary for the bitch owner to pay the stud fee at the time of the service, and that fee usually covers *only* the stud service. The written stud dog contract could also contain a guarantee that live puppies must result, or a clause stating that a second breeding will be scheduled at a subsequent heat cycle in the event of a miss. All of these details will be determined and deemed acceptable by both owners.

Each owner should evaluate the other's suitability as a business partner just as carefully as each has evaluated the other's Boxer. If the owner of the stud dog is unsure that the bitch owner is conscientious and caring, he or she should refuse the fee. Likewise, if the bitch is unworthy from the point of view of health, conformation or temperament, the breeding should not take place.

REASONS NOT TO BREED

As I said earlier, there are probably many more reasons for you *not* to breed your dog or bitch than there are reasons to do so. In addition to overpopulation, expense, and the time and energy required to be a second mother to your litter of demanding pups, there are also more health risks to Boxers used for breeding. For example, pregnancy and delivery involve risk. Cancers of the reproductive organs are more common among "intact" Boxers—mammary, uterine and testicular tumors, among others. The act of breeding may transmit infection or disease.

Spaying or neutering your Boxer also offers some benefits. In the case of the territorial male

Boxer, for instance, neutering may serve to make him more friendly to other dogs and less of an aggressor in certain doggy situations.

Neutered Boxers of both sexes can still be shown in all AKC-sponsored events with the exception of the conformation ring. However, remember that neutering is forever and is not always effective if performed on an adult to remedy a specific behavior problem. Not long ago I placed a beautiful, intact male puppy in a nonbreeding home because he had a mild heart murmur. The murmur eventually disappeared, and the dog was declared medically sound and healthy. Just as I exulted in the fact that this exceptional animal, which I still co-owned, could be shown and possibly bred, the owners informed me that their veterinarian had neutered the dog because he sporadically piddled on their new white carpets—surely the dog would cease this behavior after the surgery. I was devastated. Of course, this violation of housetraining was the result of a bad habit the pup learned when young that was never corrected properly. And the habit persists to this day.

NOTES ON NEONATES

If you're the owner of the mother-to-be, you need to prepare for the whelping. First, you need a whelping box. You can easily build a wooden one—even if you're an untalented amateur carpenter (trust me!). We use plywood. The whelping box should be approximately 3 feet by 4 feet and have sides that will accommodate height extensions to keep exploring youngsters inside as they grow larger.

The whelping box is the place where the Boxer mother will have her puppies. (S. Abraham)

Initially, our box is approximately 12 inches high, and the bitch can easily hop in and out. Some people build a small rail about halfway up from the bottom around the inside of the box so that the bitch theoretically cannot pin a puppy against the box and accidentally crush it. I haven't found this to be necessary, though; I've tried it, and my own pups have been pinned against this rail and needed rescuing on occasion anyway. We cover the floor of the box with linoleum, which can easily be sponged clean. At whelping time, we lay overlapping sheets of flat newspaper over the linoleum.

After the pups are born, we soon add shredded newspapers in the box to absorb liquids as the puppies grow. Check that the depth is reasonable so that the pups do not get lost in the newsprint. I have always avoided blankets and towels for fear that the whelps may get caught in this relatively heavy material.

The bitch should be encouraged to deliver her pups in the whelping box, or else she is sure to want to deposit them in your bedclothes. Place the box in a draft-free place where the bitch can get some privacy. She will not appreciate anyone but the immediate family near her babies in the first few weeks of life—this is not a time to have the neighborhood children over for show-and-tell.

Be sure to have a thermometer on hand, some sewing thread to tie off umbilical cords, relatively dull scissors to cut the cords, and Betadine to flush the cut cords and prevent infection. Newborn puppies need to be kept very warm. We suspend an ordinary 100-watt lightbulb over the box at a height of about 4 feet. Ambient temperatures should be 84° to 86°F at the minimum for the first two weeks of life. Many experts advocate even higher temperatures, but I don't think that's necessary. Bitches pant when they let their milk down, so do not assume that panting is a sign of stress in the new mother. During this time, the bitch should be allowed to leave the box if she chooses. While she will be loath to do so at first, sensible mothers will leave their whelps at varying intervals after the first few days, taking care to make sure that they are well fed and clean.

MILK SUPPLEMENTATION

Not all bitches produce enough milk to feed their families, especially as the growing pups make more demands of their dam. Neonates should appear round and firm to you, not thin and lanky—a sign that they are not getting enough to eat. Puppies should gain weight daily, doubling their weight by about 7 to 10 days of age. You should have a kitchen scale or a postal scale on hand to weigh the pups daily. If they are losing weight, become weak or fail to nurse, you will need to supplement their diet in order to save their lives. Check the bitch's milk supply by gently squeezing her nipples to see if she has enough milk to give. If pups are fussing and crying—even though they've nursed—they may not be getting enough nourishment. Healthy newborns do very little except eat, sleep and make the involuntary muscle movements (activated sleep) that are a sign of good health. Sick and failing puppies fail to "twitch" in this way, and this is often an early sign of a problem.

Supplementation requires either tube feeding or bottle feeding. Tube feeding is easier if you have a large litter because the feeding goes so much faster that way. You can purchase tube-feeding equipment from kennel supply houses or veterinarians. Many breeders are uncomfortable with tube feeding because it is possible to drown the puppy if the tube is inserted into a lung and not into the stomach. However, if you measure correctly from the tip of the nose to the last rib, mark the tube at that point, and then insert the tube only to that mark, you will not have to worry. The tube will slide easily over the tongue and down the throat. Just be sure to depress the plunger of the syringe *slowly*, and do not inject air.

Some pups are too weak to nurse from a bottle, and tube feeding may literally be the only way to save their lives. Eye-droppers are better than nothing but usually are not satisfactory. If you use a bottle, be sure to have a nipple with an opening suitable for the puppy's mouth—milk should not flow too fast or too slowly. I use a commercial human baby-bottle nipple made for normal newborns in the first 1 to 3 months of life.

There are many bitch's milk replacers on the market. I prefer Esbilac liquid for ease of administration and the results that I get. Many breeders swear by goat's milk. Weak puppies are often just low on blood sugar (hypoglycemic), and they may respond almost immediately to the administration of a little sugar water—warm water mixed with either honey or table sugar so that it is sweet to the taste. Do not hesitate to add some sugar-water to the prepared formula if you think a puppy will benefit. Contrary to the opinion of some breeders, I have found that many pups who require rather heroic measures in regard to supplementation do very well and lead normal adult lives. Their lives are well worth saving if you can.

It is not easy to determine the exact amount of formula to feed a newborn puppy. Basically, during the first week of life, a 1-pound puppy needs approximately 60 to 70 calories per day (not at each feeding). Esbilac contains about 1 calorie per cubic centimeter (cc or ml). Feedings should be given every 2 to 3 hours (yes, all day long) for the first few days. Follow the directions on your formula replacement container. Basically, I let a hungry puppy eat what he wishes, but when bottle feeding, I usually remove the bottle when the pup starts to slacken his intake—I don't want to overfeed and possibly cause colic. If puppies seem ravenously hungry after their previous feeding, use your common sense and increase their intake accordingly. Keep a close eye on a puppy who is nursing from a bottle, lest he choke because of

overzealous efforts to feed. Remember that not all puppies follow "manufacturer's directions" exactly—all metabolisms are not the same. So if a puppy looks too thin to your eyes, it probably is. Trust your best instincts.

A WORD ABOUT COLOR

Whether breeders admit it or not, many of us begin to select our so-called show prospects when they are just a few hours old. Excited telephone calls back and forth to friends proudly broadcast how many flashy pups were born. The plain pups, who may easily deserve to be the modest stars of the future, are often relegated to second-class citizenship and sold as pets. Recent years have witnessed a blurring of these prejudices, but they die hard. The fact that a plain fawn bitch won WB and BW at the ABC National in 1999 may do much to encourage less of a love affair with flash—which is, after all, mere window dressing and has almost nothing to do with the quality of the animal. In fact, too much white is a distraction and can be very unattractive, if not disqualifying, under the breed Standard.

White or near-white puppies are common in litters where breeders seek flash. In most instances, they are as healthy and sound as their littermates. On occasion, they may prove to be deaf. Long-held traditional custom encouraged that they be euthanized at birth. At present, ABC members are urged not to sell or register white puppies (see appendix B). However, whites may be placed in pet homes, and they are often shown in AKC performance events.

White or nearly white puppies are common in Boxer litters, though they are not allowed to be shown according to the Boxer Standard. (S. Abraham)

White pups, though they should not be bred, make wonderful pets. (S. Abraham)

A FINAL PERSPECTIVE

No phase of Boxer ownership is more fraught with heartache and joy as is the breeding and rearing of a litter. Those of us who are still seeking the mythic perfection of the Standard will probably continue to breed as long as we are able. Some will have large kennels; some will keep numbers slim and never have so many dogs that they all (and you) can't sleep on the bed at one time! Whether or not you choose to follow this path is a decision that you should not make lightly. The health, well-being, and happiness of the Boxer who loves you depends on your wise choices.

(K. Buckley)

CHAPTER 12

Caring for the Older Boxer

S ooner or later, the beloved pet you raised from puppyhood—the dog who gave you your first big thrill in the show or obedience ring, who flies to your side when you call, who looks at you with "those eyes," who grew up with your children—begins to slow down. The signs may be subtle and insidious, but also inexorable. Time waits for no living creature.

The elderly Boxer is a treasure—a great gift that you should hold dear. He must not feel as though the new hopeful has taken his special place in your home or your heart. At the same time, it is your responsibility to recognize the tell-tale signs that his age is advancing so you can take appropriate measures to enrich and prolong your Boxer's happy life.

SIGNS OF AGING

All Boxers do not age at the same rate in the same way. But gradually, certain signs do appear in most—some sooner, some later. One of the earliest signs to look for is the tell-tale flecking of gray on the black of the mask. If you have a dog with a particularly flashy muzzle, you can see this occurring in the black around the eyes and sometimes on the face in general. I tend to notice this in my own dogs at about 7 years old, and it is not at all indicative of longevity. Some dogs gray early and live long lives, and some do not. But it is a sort of wake-up call for us to take special care of our senior citizen. Your Boxer won't think of himself as a canine elder, though. He'll be willing to romp and play and do far more than is perhaps in his best interests. So it's imperative that you, as his owner, use some common sense and recognize when to pay attention to advancing years.

Gradual Hearing Loss

At some point, your Boxer's hearing may become less acute. The dog who once jumped to his feet at the lightest of footfalls may remain asleep on his rug now. He may not respond as readily to your calls; he isn't ignoring you, he simply doesn't hear you. An odd benefit to this is that any sensitivity to the sound of rumbling thunder will vanish from your Boxer's world when he can no longer register sound in that decibel range. As hearing acuity diminishes, it may become even more imperative than usual to walk your dog on a leash because he may not hear you if danger threatens.

Even though your Boxer is getting along in years, he should still remain trim. Here, the sleek Ch. CJ's Silver Exchange has placed in the Veteran's Class at the National Specialty. (Ashbey)

Changes in Weight

The sight of a fat boxer is an unhappy one, whether he is young or old. As your dog exercises less with age, he will not need as many calories to sustain himself. It is incumbent on you to adjust his food quantity and quality properly to compensate for his naturally slower metabolic rate. Decrease in thyroid function may also predispose him to weight gain. Conversely, many medical conditions may cause weight loss—certain cancers, for example, diabetes or Cushing's Disease. Any marked departure from your Boxer's normal eating habits or any sudden change in his overall condition should be checked by a veterinarian.

Arthritis

Many Boxers develop osteoarthritis with age. This is a degenerative and common joint disease. Your dog may evince pain and stiffness when rising from a nap or overdoing his romps in the yard. Sudden changes in weather may bring on symptoms. Affected dogs may become reluctant to jump and run as time progresses. Occasionally they can develop spondylosis, an osteoarthritis of the spine. They may become intolerant of especially rambunctious children who don't realize that, try as he might, their elder Boxer can no longer tolerate their rough play with impunity. Luckily, veterinary science has made great strides to treat the discomfort of such conditions with a variety of pain-killing, anti-inflammatory medications. Some of the most effective bear the trade names Rimadyl and Cosequin. These have many of the advantages of the steroids without some of their unpleasant side effects.

Any sudden evidence of a joint problem, especially if associated with a low-grade fever, may be indicative of Lyme Disease, now widespread throughout much of the United States. Your veterinarian may recommend a prophylactic course of appropriate antibiotics if he suspects this tick-borne disease. In our area of Connecticut, where Lyme is endemic, any painful joint ill is routinely treated as Lyme until proven otherwise. Unfortunately, Lyme titres may test negative in the early stages. Diagnosis is often empirical.

Cardiac Problems

Of course, as with a younger dog, any middle-aged to older Boxer who suffers spells of weakness, fainting or collapse must be examined thoroughly to rule out the possibility of cardiomyopathy (see chapter 6). Fortunately, it is no longer necessarily a death sentence, and a positive diagnosis means that most owners will have the opportunity to treat their Boxer with anti-arrhythmic medication that may greatly lengthen his life. I have known of dogs to live more than four excellent years on such medications until they are lost to other unrelated illnesses. Subaortic stenosis may also cause fainting and weakness; your cardiologist can distinguish readily between the two conditions.

The dilated form of cardiomyopathy, wear and tear on the valves, or any possible resistance in the arteries may predispose your Boxer to eventual heart failure. The lungs and abdomen may fill with fluid. Medications such as Vasotec and digitalis can

Ten-year-old littermates Kaiya's Tigre and Kaiya's Reckless Rascal are enjoying their golden years together. (D-J MacWhinnie)

Bert at 2 years old.

Bert at 12½ years old. (E. Mangiafico)

help to dilate the blood vessels and aid the heart to pump more effectively and with less effort.

Failing Eyesight

Generally, a Boxer's eyesight will remain acute all his life. But a gradual clouding of the lenses is a normal part of the aging process and not unusual. Cataracts are not common in the breed but may develop as years advance. Unfortunately, cataract removal in the canine is a much less reliable process than it is in humans. Ulcers of the cornea, while not unique to the aging Boxer, are sometimes refractory to treatment at any age. Sudden evidence of eye pain—squinting, pawing and rubbing—should be investigated by your veterinarian. Usually, a nonsteroid antibiotic ointment applied topically will aid the healing process. In more severe cases, an ophthalmologist may apply a collagen patch to help the corneal repair.

Dental Problems

Especially as your Boxer ages, it is necessary to check his teeth and gums regularly and maintain proper dental hygiene. The elder dog's teeth will be noticeably worn down and sometimes seem to disappear into the gums themselves. This is a perfectly natural part of the aging process.

Recall from chapter 6 that the breed is prone to gingival hyperplasia, a benign overgrowth of gum tissue, often beginning in middle age. This may cause food particles to catch and remain in the mouth long enough to promote tooth decay. Rarely, this gum tissue may need to be removed to prevent constant irritation and bleeding. Usually, though, however unsightly, it can be left alone. Regular mouthwash with a canine decay preventive is advisable. If tartar builds up to the extent that your veterinarian wants to clean the teeth under anesthesia, your Boxer should undergo a course of prophylactic antibiotics prior to and after this procedure to prevent bacteria from the mouth from entering the bloodstream and possibly causing heart damage. Always be sure that you are comfortable with whatever anesthesia your veterinarian proposes to use.

The older Boxer's teeth may predispose to tartar formation, often noticeable at the gum line as a yellow-brown deposit. A tooth scaler will help to remove any especially noticeable buildup that may foster infection and disease, but excessive tartar is not often a severe problem.

At 10½, Jessa deserves to enjoy the more sedentary life of a retiree. (E. Mangiafico)

Dental checkups will reveal any unexpected tumors that may possibly be malignant. Always have any suspicious lesions in the mouth checked as soon as possible, as oral cancers are often aggressive in nature.

DIET FOR THE SENIOR CITIZEN

The elder Boxer may greatly benefit from the kibble foods specially formulated for dogs over the age of 7 years. Specifically, they address the needs of the canine senior citizen—the dog whose body cells decline faster than the body can repair or replace them. Nutritional scientists have spent years formulating such dog foods. Some of the research has revealed that dogs, along with people, naturally lose some muscle mass as they age.

At the age of 9½, Ch. Trefoil's Caruso retains the smooth coat and clean musculature of a younger dog. Only the white of his once-black mask reveals his age. (S. Abraham)

Remember that even the youthful Boxer is never particularly tolerant of extremes of heat or cold, so please see to it that your aging dog is kept warm and dry in the winter and safe from excessive heat in the summertime.

EXERCISE

Old Boxers, like old owners, slow down over time. You may observe that your dog just doesn't want to tear around the yard with his toys with the same abandon of his youth. He may lie down and play more sedately. Pay attention to what your pet is telling you because if you insist on throwing a ball for his normal half hour, he will still try to oblige.

It's up to you to recognize that your Boxer doesn't want or need this prolonged activity any more. That doesn't mean that it is normal for him to curl up and do nothing—that would be cause for concern. Rather, his old bones and joints and muscles are telling him to take it easier—and he is telling you.

Many older Boxers are capable of amazing feats, such as 8- and 9-year-olds entering the Agility or Obedience ring for the first time or continuing a fine career—with great success. But these same dogs might tire on a strenuous five-mile hike, so be watchful and temper the exercise regimen to suit your dog's senior status.

Walking is still wonderful exercise for both humans and their canine companions. Your Boxer looks forward to a daily walk with great anticipation, always ready to surprise a squirrel or just to have the one-on-one time with you, his most important person. Good brisk walks for distances that are comfortable are wonderful for promoting good cardiovascular health, and they also serve to keep muscles and joints up to par.

VETERINARY CARE

Inoculations must not be neglected just because your Boxer is aging. However, some practitioners recommend longer intervals between boosters than in the younger animal. Ask your veterinarian for advice. Regular checkups are very important to monitor heart and general condition. Once every six months is not too frequent to have the senior citizen examined by a good practitioner. The veterinarian who treated your dog as a puppy and knows him best will be a great asset in assessing his condition as he grows older.

Some veterinarians recommend yearly blood-test profiles to keep watch for hidden dangers before they surface. These results may reveal health issues that can be treated more effectively because they are caught early. Significant advances in canine geriatric medicine may mean years of good life left because a potentially life-threatening problem was evaluated and treated before it became critical.

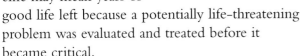

At 9 years old, Tokalon's Fuerstin sails over the Single-Bar Jump at an Agility Trial. (TienTran Photography)

HOLISTIC APPROACHES

A number of dog fanciers have a strong belief in the value of homeopathic medicine. Increasingly, homeopathic veterinarians are to be found in all areas of the United States. For those Boxer owners who have concerns that vaccinations may compromise an aging immune system or who simply believe in a more holistic approach to curing disease at any age, the homeopath may prove to be a great ally. Canine acupuncture, chiropractic care, massage and nutritional therapy and herbal and homeopathic medicines just might be appropriate for some aging Boxers. Such so-called alternative approaches are increasingly finding their way into mainstream medical practice.

INTRODUCING A NEW PUPPY

If you have not already done so, you may choose at some point to introduce a young puppy or adult into the household. This is a perfectly logical decision, but one that must be handled carefully. Don't let the new arrival overwhelm your faithful older friend. Keep a close eye on them at first to make sure there is no animosity on the part of the elder dog or bitch. The adult may or may not take kindly to a bouncy bundle of puppy joy, continually in the face, the food and the toys that belonged exclusively to the senior dog. It is up to you to carefully assess the situation and stop any trouble before it starts. Remember that most Boxers do not love to share your affection with other animals of any species, and it will be important for you to give equal time to the 10-year-old while you are housetraining a puppy. If you have a retired show dog, make an extra effort during this adjustment period to include him in your weekend travels or take extra time with him on walks or playtime. Do not make him feel as though he has been neglected or tossed aside in favor of the new arrival.

When introducing a youngster into the household, it is best to do it away from any blankets, beds or special toys that the older dog holds especially

At nearly 9 years old, Ch. Trefoil's Choirmaster adopts the familiar Boxer pose that says: Try and take it from me if you can! (S. Abraham)

dear. A meeting outside of the confines of the house would be ideal. Under no circumstances should you allow the puppy near the food dish of the adult, as the most even-tempered of Boxers may take exception to a puppy who does not know his manners. In short, use your common sense. In time, most adult Boxers will accept a puppy or young adult (of the opposite sex) in the home. They may even become great friends, and your careful monitoring of their exercise and play may also help to keep the old dog young beyond his years.

EUTHANASIA

Good-bye is the most difficult word to say. But there may come a time when illness or pain requires you to make the most wrenching and difficult of decisions. Make no mistake: "Putting to sleep," while it may be the kindest thing, is just a euphemism for death. When that dreaded time comes, a loving owner will know that he is doing what is best for his pet, to end suffering, to take the pain out of his Boxer's eyes. Search your heart thoroughly to make sure that you are doing this because you care for your dog, not your own convenience.

If you have a veterinarian who will perform the procedure at your home, so much the better. It is a kindness that the dog does not have to be bundled into a car and driven to a clinic that he may never have cared for during the best of times. But wherever the euthanasia is performed, I could not imagine being absent. As difficult as it is for us, we owe our dogs the reassurance of our touch and our voice. I have held several dogs over the years, gently, with their heads in my lap, while the veterinarian administered the intra-

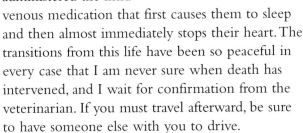

Your older Boxer may not take kindly to a young puppy entering the household. Then again, they may become great friends. (K. Ontell)

venous medication that first causes them to sleep and then almost immediately stops their heart. The transitions from this life have been so peaceful in every case that I am never sure when death has intervened, and I wait for confirmation from the veterinarian. If you must travel afterward, be sure to have someone else with you to drive.

If your local ordinances allow, and you have the land, you may elect to bury your dog in a favorite spot on your property—perhaps under a tree or in a garden where you shared many happy hours with your Boxer. Or you may elect to have

your dog cremated and the remains returned to you; you must specifically request a private cremation if you wish to keep the ashes. This will cost a bit more, but it may provide you with some peace of mind at a very difficult time.

When the end does come, allow yourself to grieve. It is normal and natural that you do so. But remember that, for all the reasons you loved your Boxer in life, you owe it to yourself to share your days with another Boxer if you haven't already made that decision. It is a kind of tribute to your lost companion that you live on with another. No two dogs are alike, and it would be unfair for you to try to cast a second dog in the exact mold of the first. Boxers, like people, all have their great virtues. When you think of the love you once knew, you will recognize that you have enjoyed quite a remarkable journey. Do not hesitate to embark on another—different, but no less to be cherished.

Ch. TuRo's Cachet. (J. Ashbey)

The American Boxer Club

On February 16, 1935, the newly fledged American Boxer Club held its first recorded meeting in New York City and applied for AKC membership in March. The AKC granted the request in May of the same year. Names on the original membership roster read like a "Who's Who" of Boxerdom—Harold and Lillian Palmedo (Harold was President), Mr. and Mrs. Alexander Nitt, Mrs. Ida Gaertner, Dr. Clinton Barker, Mrs. Arthur Lewis, Miss Marcia Fennessey (Cirrol Kennels), Mrs. L. W. Whittemore, F. Greenhagen, A. V. Barber, John and Mazie Wagner (Mazelaine Kennels), Miriam Breed (Barmere Kennels), Max Ketzel, Mrs. Durfee and Walter and Katherine Lippert (Hinschenfeld Kennels).

Almost at once, the club petitioned the AKC to move the Boxer from the Non-Sporting Group to the Working Group, and in September the Boxer became an official Working Dog, a status it enjoys to this day. The *AKC Gazette* pictured Ch. Sigurd vom Dom of Barmere on its July cover—the first Boxer to appear as a cover dog. Mrs. Arthur Lewis wrote the breed column for the *Gazette* and covered topics relating to club doings, obedience, parasites and ear cropping.

On June 6, 1936, the ABC held its first National Specialty in conjunction with the Greenwich Kennel Club at Port Chester, New York. Thirty-five Boxers participated, and the BOB winner was Ch. Corso v. Uracher Wasserfall se Sumbula, an import owned by the Palmedos. He repeated this triumph the following year. The Wagners' German import, Ich Dorian v. Marienhof of Mazelaine, won BOB at

Westminster in 1936, and then the Working Group there in 1937. He won twenty-two all-breed Best in Shows, then a record for the breed.

Confusion and controversy surrounded the wording of the official breed Standard. One club faction favored a version permitting no white markings above the line of the shoulder, and complicated and exacting measurements of head and body proportions. In 1938, the Standard was revised after Philip Stockmann (Vom Dom Kennels) and Jack Wagner worked for hours on it one night in a hotel room in New York City. Herr Stockmann, Chief German Breed Warden, was in the United States because he was judging an unprecedented entry of 102 Boxers at Westminster. Before the night was out, the revised Standard forbade Checks (over ⅓ white), but permitted flash. The complex measurements of body and head were largely deleted. The present breed Standard still embraces the principles and even contains much of the wording of this pioneering effort. By the end of 1938, membership in the ABC stood at 106, and 724 Boxers had been

Ch. Wagner's Wilverday Famous Amos, SOM, is the only Boxer ever to win Best of Breed four times at the ABC National Specialty. (J. Ashbey)

registered individually with the AKC.

Today, the American Boxer Club enjoys a rich geographical diversity, with 56 member clubs and an eclectic individual membership roster of 900. The club is active in many endeavors and dedicated to the betterment of the Boxer breed in the home, in the Show and Obedience ring, in Agility and in all the other aspects of the Boxer's life and times.

THE ABC SPECIALTY

Since 1936, the American Boxer Club has held an annual Specialty to which dedicated Boxer enthusiasts travel from all over the nation. From that initial entry of 35 in Greenwich, Connecticut, they have expanded to 647 Boxers shown in Conformation in Frederick, Maryland, in 1999. In 1957, the ABC Regional Specialty was born—a rotating Specialty designed to accommodate ABC members who live far away from the ABC National.

Held in conjunction with the National, the Futurity began in 1945. It is open to Boxers

18 months of age or younger whose dams were nominated to the Futurity before they whelped. Each Futurity entrant is then individually nominated on or before his 4-month birthday. The Futurity is a real breeder's showcase, and cash prizes—some substantial—are awarded to the winners. No AKC points are involved, but the prestige is considerable: 249 Boxers competed in the Futurity in 1999.

At present, the ABC events are held over a six-day period during the second week of May. In 1999, there were sixty-five Obedience entries, and Agility was offered for the first time. Obedience was held from 1947 to 1972 (no trial in 1971) when it was discontinued; it was revived in 1995.

Judges for the Futurity and the classes are elected by the ABC membership two years in advance of the show. It is considered a great honor to be selected by such a critical peer group.

Ch. Holly Lane's Crème de Menthe was best of Opposite Sex at the 1999 ABC National under Judge David Abraham. (Nutting)

ABC AWARDS

The ABC gives out a number of awards each year, including rewards for those Boxers achieving the most outstanding show records for the previous year, those breeding the most champions and so on. Among the most coveted awards are those relating to Sires and Dams of Merit. A SOM must have sired seven or more AKC champions, while a DOM must have produced at least four AKC champions. The even more-rarefied Legion of Merit winners have produced Producers—four SOM/DOM for males and three SOM/DOM for females. At present, there are only three Legion of Merit dams and thirty-two Legion of Merit sires in breed history.

The Larry Downey Award has been offered since 1978 to honor people who have made outstanding efforts on behalf of the American Boxer Club. In 1999, the presentation was made to Frances Abercrombie.

TOP TWENTY

The Top Twenty Boxers (as determined by the number of dogs defeated in breed competition during the prior calendar year) compete at the ABC National Specialty for Top Twenty honors. Three judges—a breeder, a breeder-judge and a

This remarkable photograph was reproduced as a poster to raise money for rescue activities. It was taken by Tracy Hendrickson, Chairman and Founder of the American Boxer Rescue Association.

Kriste Kaemmlein is shown winning Best Junior Handler at the 1999 ABC National Specialty, showing Stony Crest of Thunder Ridge. Kriste was also Best Junior Handler at the World Dog Show in Mexico that same year. (Nutting)

THE AMERICAN BOXER CHARITABLE FOUNDATION, INC.

The ABCF was founded in 1995 by a concerned group of fanciers and ABC members. This nonprofit foundation seeks to obtain donations toward medical research in areas of special concern to the Boxer. The health and welfare of the breed is its primary concern. Fund-raisers are held across the country—dinners, auctions, bake sales and raffles have funded the efforts of the ABCF. The American Boxer Club has itself donated $5000 for each of the past two years. Monies have come from foreign countries, notably and with thanks, from the Boxer Club of Canada. All bequests and donations are tax deductible, as the foundation has received tax-exempt status from the U.S. Internal Revenue Service.

One recent donation from the ABCF was $25,000 to the American Kennel Club's Canine Health Foundation. These funds were earmarked for research into Boxer Cardiomyopathy by Dr. Kate Meurs at Ohio State University. Several other research projects are currently under review. The ABCF is proud that it is to date the largest single-breed club contributor to the AKC Canine Health Foundation, with donations totaling $117,500. Since the AKC generously matches breed club donations, that amounted to a significant sum to support vital programs.

multibreed judge—evaluate the dogs in a complex system of scoring that enables one animal to emerge with the highest point total on one memorable evening during ABC week. Judges' names are kept top secret until Top Twenty night. Handlers and judges participate in formal dress, and it is quite a gala occasion. The Top Twenty winner in 1999 was Ch. Storybook's Rip It Up, handled by Michael Shepherd and owned by Cheryl and Keith Robbins of Georgia.

*Awards of Excellence are coveted honors at the ABC.
Pictured is the fawn bitch Ch. Champagne Touched By An
Angel with handler Jennifer Gelinas. (Nutting)*

*Ch. Carlon's Red Hot was Winner's Bitch, Best of Winners
and Best of Opposite Sex at the 1995 ABC National under
judge Stephanie Abraham. (Nutting)*

BREED RESCUE

The ABC encourages and supports rescue efforts on
many fronts. The ABC's Rescue Coordinator in
Broken Arrow, Oklahoma, Tracy Hendrickson, is
part of a network of dedicated volunteers across the
United States. Often, veterinarians and other professionals also donate their time and expertise to aid
these rescue efforts. Placement of abandoned, abused
or unwanted Boxers is truly a labor of love, with
untold hours and a good amount of money devoted
to the rehabilitation and re-homing of deserving
animals. Dogs must be housed, fed, treated for medical ailments and eventually spayed or neutered in

most instances. With Boxer popularity on the
rise—and over 35,000 Boxers being registered
yearly by the AKC—there will be more and more
need for rescue placement. The heartwarming stories of successful placements are legion. For me,
one of the most poignant involved the loving family that adopted a 12-year-old guide dog bitch
who had been abandoned to the pound because
she could no longer perform her duties effectively.
Hard to believe, but true. She lived out her days
with dignity and the adoring affection of her new
family.

Those with rescue donations, those willing to
work in rescue efforts or those looking for a rescued

Ch. Hi-Tech's Johnny J of Boxerton, winner in 1997 and 1998 of the ABC's BOB at the National Specialty, shown here with Kim Pastella. (J. Ashbey)

Am./Can. Ch. Sirrocco's Kiss By the Book. (J. Ashbey)

Boxer, are advised to contact the ABC member club in your area for referral. Telephone numbers and links to e-mail addresses are available at several Internet sites and in appendix A.

PUBLICATIONS

There are a number of books about the Boxer in the marketplace. Most of them are valuable additions to the library of anyone truly interested in learning more about this remarkable breed. The American Boxer Club Historian, at present Eleanor Linderholm Wood, keeps a record of the ABC over the years and can direct you to pertinent club publications as well as other seminal works.

One book of great historical interest, which is out of print but still available at many second-hand bookshops, is John P. Wagner's classic *The Boxer*, copyright 1953 by Orange Judd Publishing Co. (see "Bibliography"). This work offers great historical insight into the progenitors of the modern Boxer; discusses anatomy, judging and breeding; and affords a wealth of photographs that can be found nowhere else.

The other classic work that no true Boxer enthusiast should be without is *My Life With Boxers* by Friederun von Miram-Stockmann. Mrs. Stockmann, of Vom Dom Kennels fame in Germany, exported three of the four foundation sires to the United States in the 1930s. Her chronicle of the establishment of her kennel and bloodlines in war-torn Germany is fascinating and of considerable historical value to students of the breed. Originally published in Germany in 1960, it is now available in a new English translation by Calvin D. Gruver, an ABC member, and is published by Classic Pet Books (see "Bibliography"). A limited edition, it has been offered as a gift for donors to the American Boxer Club Charitable Foundation, Inc., but it is available for sales as well. ABC members receive a quarterly *Bulletin* which is filled with current, salient breed information. The *American Kennel Club Gazette* publishes a Boxer breed column on a quarterly basis; the subject matter is timely and informative.

Ch. Huffland's Obladah of Arriba, Top Twenty Winner and ABC Best of Opposite Sex, 1998. (M. Adams)

Ch. Merrilane's Knockout shown here winning BOB at East Bay Boxer Club. (Callea Photo)

The ABC offers a brochure intended as an introduction to the breed, complete with color and sepia/white photographs. Titled "Meet the Boxer," it is available for a very nominal sum from the club—contact the corresponding secretary. In addition, an "Illustrated Standard of the Breed" is also available, written and illustrated by Eleanor Linderholm Wood of Merrilane Boxers. Intended for breeders and judges, it is an excellent resource for any serious Boxer enthusiast.

EDUCATION

Increasingly, the ABC is being called upon to educate breeders, judges and the public at large.

Ch. Rochil's Grand Marshall. (Sunrise Photo)

Every year at the National Specialty, a Breeders' and Judges' Seminar is held. This program includes slides and a discussion led by respected breeders and judges, with the opportunity for hands-on examination of individual dogs. A Health Seminar is also offered. In 1999, this program focused on skin tumors and Boxer Cardiomyopathy. ABC members across the country can access any information the parent club can provide to hold regional seminars when requested.

Breeder referrals are provided through ABC member clubs. The public is encouraged to contact these local club representatives for help in acquiring a Boxer puppy or adult.

The American Boxer Club is responsible for the written breed Standard. All amendments to the Standard must be ratified by a vote of the ABC membership and approved by the AKC. In 1998, a proposal to include a description of the natural ear was defeated in a club vote. In 1999, a revision to this Standard, meant to clarify judging protocols, was added as its last line (see Chapter 3). The AKC mandates that changes to breed Standards can be made only once every five years. Therefore, no further revisions can appear before the year 2004.

Epilogue

Since the day in 1953 when my parents purchased a "plain" fawn bitch puppy named Duchess just for me, I have been involved with Boxers. My close childhood friend was the daughter of the president of the American Boxer Club, and I can still remember many happy hours playing on the floor of Robert and Doris Bunshaft's living room with their Rogue Hill Boxers. Duchess lived a long life—into my college days—and it wasn't too many years later that I married. Together, my husband and I set out to find a dog and ended up in 1970—with blinding good fortune—with a Boxer who was one of the finest of his generation.

As Trefoil Boxers, we have always been a small home kennel, and the dogs live in our home as house pets first and show dogs second. Because of restricted space and a husband who is far more practical than I, we have sold many a good dog because there are only so many places on the couch! I have always enjoyed handling my own dogs in the ring, and although not blessed with great natural talent in this regard, I have become competent enough to finish the titles of several of my own Boxers. We have not hesitated to employ the "pros" when I was unable to get the job done adequately on my own. Not every dog wants to work for "Mother!"

In 1982, I became an AKC judge and still enjoy this role immensely. It was a great honor and thrill to judge Bitches and Intersex at the American Boxer Club National in 1995. I am presently Head of Judges' Education and Publicity for the American Boxer Club and have written the *AKC Gazette* Boxer column (with a brief interruption) since the early 1990s. I am serving my third term on the ABC Board of Directors. Because I have lost Boxers to both cancer and cardiomyopathy, I have a great interest in the research being done to help our dogs live longer and fuller lives. I am happy to report that Boxer breeders are becoming more and more aware of health concerns and are doing their best to breed away from inherited problems whenever possible. Funding from the American Boxer Club Charitable Foundation, matched by the American Kennel Club, is supporting research critical to the well-being of the breed.

The 1990s, unfortunately, witnessed a great deal of breed-specific anti-dog legislation being introduced into state and municipal government. The Boxer is sometimes named on lists of so-called dangerous breeds—lists compiled by people who obviously never owned or knew a Boxer in

The author's childhood pet, Diligent Duchess, was sired by champion Mazelaine Keynote. (S. Abraham)

their lives. The ignorant among us sometimes mistake the Boxer for a Pit Bull, often with tragic consequences for the Boxer.

It is imperative that Boxer owners, perhaps working in conjunction with Boxer clubs, educate their local animal shelters, civic organizations and schools as to what a Boxer is and is not. It is truly ironic that the Boxer, whose disposition is usually superlative, may legally be considered to be a threat to some communities.

I hope that you have enjoyed the preceding pages. Most of all, I hope that reading this book has helped you to better understand and care for the dog that means so much to you. Your relationship with your Boxer, and his unique relationship to you and your family, will undoubtedly remain a highlight of your life.

(R. Zurflieh)

Resources

ORGANIZATIONS

American Boxer Club (ABC)

American Boxer Club (ABC)
Mrs. Barbara Wagner, Secretary
6310 Edward Dr.
Clinton, MD 20735
www.akc.org/clubs/abc/abc-home.htm

American Boxer Club Charitable Foundation
Bruce Korson, President
c/o P.O. Box 300
Rockwood, MI 48173-0300
(734) 676-9063
Fax: (734) 692-8991

American Boxer Club Rescue
Tracy Hendrickson, Coordinator
4412 W. Kent Circle
Broken Arrow, OK 74012
(918) 250-9004
Additional Rescue contacts at AKC Web site (see above entry)

American Kennel Club (AKC)

American Kennel Club (AKC)
5580 Centerview Dr.
Raleigh, NC 27606
(919) 233-9767

Ch. Jaquet's Noire. (G. Glazbrook)

The American Boxer Club's Code of Ethics

This CODE OF ETHICS (Articles I through IV) is set forth as a guideline to protect and advance the interests of Boxers and to encourage sportsmanlike competition at dog shows, obedience trials and tracking events, including a respect for people and dogs. It is presented as a guideline for American Boxer Club members to follow when breeding, buying, selling or competing and exhibiting their Boxers.

Members of the American Boxer Club will conduct themselves in such a manner as to reflect credit on the sport of purebred dogs and on Boxers in particular, regardless of the location or circumstances.

AKC Rules and Regulations and THE AMERICAN BOXER CLUB BY-LAWS should be known and adhered to at all times. It is important to know the current Standard of the Breed.

ARTICLE I

Breeding

1. Breed only with the intention of improving the breed.

2. Breed only from healthy, sound, typey individuals who display good sound temperament and qualities, which are free of known disqualifying faults.

3. All dogs offered at stud should be in good health. They should be free from Canine Brucellosis and other communicable diseases as well as disqualifying genetic faults. A written Stud Contract is essential and it should state that the owner of the Stud Dog will not sign a litter registration application which includes in the count any puppies with a color disqualification (Art. 5. Page 4). Monorchids are not considered breeding stock.

4. Any bitch accepted for stud service should be at least eighteen months of age, in good health, free from communicable diseases and disqualifying faults. The bitch must be accompanied by a current Veterinarian's certificate stating that she is free of Canine Brucellosis. It is the responsibility of the stud dog owner to properly provide for all visiting bitches' safety and security. Each bitch must be bred only to the stud dog specified by her owner. A change of stud dog is only permitted with the express consent of the owner of the bitch and should be included as an amendment to the Stud Contract.

5. Bitches should be bred only between the ages of eighteen months and six years and not more than once a year.

6. Breeders will keep accurate breeding papers, pedigrees and contracts.

ARTICLE II
Health and Maintenance

1. Breeders should encourage the X-raying, OFA certifying of hips, as well as testing for thyroid and other determinable conditions which would affect the health of their dogs or the offspring of same.

2. Tail docking, removal of dew claws and ear cropping are appropriate for the well-being of the Breed. Corrective cosmetic surgery will not be performed on Boxers. If and when such corrective surgery becomes a necessity, the dog will no longer be exhibited, if such alteration is not acceptable to stated AKC policies.

3. Members of The American Boxer Club will strive to maintain their Boxers' condition, health and quarters in a manner which is above reproach in every respect.

ARTICLE III
Registration

There are two ways to register puppies for the first time with the "blue registration application" slip.

1. LIMITED REGISTRATION

American Boxer Club Members are encouraged to indicate application for a limited registration for the following:

a. Boxers being purchased only as registered companion pets.

b. Boxers that are not considered sound, or not of breeding quality including monorchids.

Note: The limited registration registers the puppy; it does not allow the registration of any offspring from the mature dog. The breeder of the dog can cancel the limited registration should the puppy at maturity be considered of breeding quality.

2. FULL REGISTRATION

Register Boxers who are sound, healthy, typey, considered to be of breeding quality and are free of disqualifying faults under the Standard of the Breed (Art. 5).

ARTICLE IV

1. All sales of puppies and adults should include:

   a. AKC registration application papers

   b. Signed Bill of Sale

   c. An accurate three generation pedigree

   d. ABC Brochure and/or copy of the Standard of the Breed

   e. Health record including shots given, diet and care information

Note: Registration papers may be withheld at the time of the sale in such cases of prior agreement in writing.

Example: Spay/neuter agreement; Breeding/Lease agreement or other similar contracted agreement, which would delay transfer of ownership until completion of contract.

2. If possible, puppies should remain in their litter environment until at least seven weeks of age★ (see note on p. 200).

3. Purchasers should be urged to spay or neuter all pets.

4. Misleading or untruthful statements must not be used in the selling or advertising of puppies. Misrepresentation of American Boxer Club awards, A.K.C. and/or foreign titles must be carefully avoided.

5. American Boxer Club Members will at all times strive to be accurate and honest to the best of their ability in appraising the quality of Boxers being offered for sale or placement with reference to the Standard of the Breed.

6. All contracts must be clear and complete with any and all conditions stated. A signed copy must be provided to each party involved.

7. During the life of any Boxer sold or placed, the breeder should endeavor to help the owner in every reasonable way.

Ch. Bridgewood's B.K. Kahuna, SOM. (V. Cook)

Obedience Titles

CD	Companion Dog
CDX	Companion Dog Excellent
UD	Utility Dog
UDX	Utility Dog Excellent
OTCh	Obedience Trial Champion

Agility Titles

NA	Novice Agility
OA	Open Agility
AX	Agility Excellent
MX	Master Agility Excellent
NAJ	Novice Jumpers with Weaves
OAJ	Open Jumpers with Weaves
AXJ	Excellent Jumpers with Weaves

Tracking Titles

TD	Tracking Dog
TDX	Tracking Dog Excellent
VST	Variable Surface Tracking Dog

Combination Titles

UDT	Utility Dog Tracker
UDTX	Utility Dog Tracker Excellent

Canine Good Citizen

CGC	Canine Good Citizen

This title does not appear on certified AKC pedigrees but may be added by the owner for advertising and/or identification purposes.

North American Dog Agility Council

NAC	Novice Agility Certificate
OAC	Open Agility Certificate
EAC	Elite Agility Certificate
NATCh	Agility Champion

Gamblers and Jumpers titles are offered as well. These would be written as NGC, OGC, EGC, NJC and so on.

United States Dog Agility Association

AD	Agility Dog
AAD	Advanced Agility Dog
MAD	Masters Agility Dog
ADCH	Agility Dog Champion
SM	Snookers Masters
GM	Gamblers Masters
JM	Jumpers Masters
RM	Relay Masters
VAD	Veteran Agility Dog
AdCh	Agility Dog Champion

Schutzhund Titles

BH	*Begleithund* (Companion Dog)—entry-level title
SchH1, SchH2, SchH3	Schutzhund Protection Dog; each level more difficult than the next
IPO1, IPO2, IPO3	*Internationale Pruefungsordnung;* each level more difficult than the next (Like SchH1, SchH2 and SchH3 but with international rules that differ for protection work)
FH1, FH2	*Faehrtenhund* (Tracking Dog); each level more difficult than the next
AD	*Ausdauer* (Endurance Test)
ZTP	Breeding Suitability Test

OTHER TITLES

TDI	Therapy Dog International
TR1	Tracking One
VCC	CCC Working Registry's Versatile Canine Companion
VCCX	Versatile Canine Companion Excellent
O-VCCX	Outstanding Versatile Canine Companion

DOG SHOW ABBREVIATIONS

BIS	Best in Show
BISS	Best in Show Specialty
BOB	Best of Breed
BOS	Best of Opposite Sex
WD	Winners Dog
WB	Winners Bitch
RWD	Reserve Winners Dog
RWB	Reserve Winners Bitch
BW	Best of Winners
GR1	Group First (GR2, GR3, GR4)

OBEDIENCE ABBREVIATIONS

HIT	Highest Scoring Dog in Trial
HC	Highest Combined Scoring Dog in Trial

Ch. Kimber D. Pinebrook Dusty Road. (T. Nutting)

Boxer Notables

AMERICAN BOXER CLUB NATIONAL SPECIALTY WINNERS, 1989–99

46th Annual Specialty Show, May 7–11, 1989, Newark, NJ

BOB	Ch.Berena's Tribute to Fa–Fa Breeder/Owners: Larry and Gene Neumann and Bernie and Rena Toon
BOS	Ch.Jodi Emmy Murphy of Heritage Breeder/Owners: Jane B. Moog and Joan Johnson
Grand Prize Futurity Winner	Thanque Joy of Interlude Breeders: Jerry and Dorothy Bryant Owner: Thanque Kennels, Reg.

47th Annual Specialty Show, May 7–11, 1990, Newark, NJ

BOB   Ch. Heldenbrand's Jet Breaker
             Breeder: E. Heldenbrand
             Owner: Jeff and Shirley Bennett and Judy Hunt

BOS   Ch. Kiebla's Tradition of TuRo
             Breeder: Kitti Barker
             Owners: Bruce and Jeanne Korson, Sandy Roberts and
             Kitti Barker

Grand Prize Futurity Winner TuRo's Solitaire
             Breeder: Robert Burke, and Sandy Roberts
             Owners: Sandy Roberts, Elizabeth Esacove and
             Robert Burke

48th Annual Specialty Show, May 6–10, 1991, Newark, NJ

BOB   Ch. Kiebla's Tradition of TuRo (see 1990)

BOS   Ch. Fiero's Tally-Ho Tailo
             Breeder: Ingrid Feder
             Owners: Dr. and Mrs. William C. Truesdale

Grand Prize Futurity Winner Karmel's Dream Weaver
             Breeder/Owners: Karin and Melvin Wilson

49th Annual Specialty Show, May 4–8, 1992, Newark, NJ

BOB   Ch. Kiebla's Tradition of TuRo (see 1990)

BOS   Ch. Shieldmont's Let's Make a Deal
             Breeders: Nance W. and Richard G. Shields
             Owners: Mr. and Mrs. Judson L. Streicher

Grand Prize Futurity Winner Karmel's Calendar Girl
             Breeder/Owners: Karin and Melvin Wilson

50th Annual Specialty Show, May 10–14, 1993, Newark, NJ

BOB	Ch. Kiebla's Tradition of TuRo (see 1990)
BOS	Ch. Hi-Tech's Arbitrage Breeder: Jo Anne Sheffler Owners: Dr. and Mrs. William Truesdale
Grand Prize Futurity Winner	Ch. Hollylane's Free as the Wind Breeder: Eileen McClintock Owners: Steven G. and Ann B. Anderson

51st Annual Specialty Show, May 9–13, 1994, Newark, NJ

BOB	Ch. Hi-Tech's Arbitrage (see 1993)
BOS	Ch. Kiebla's Tradition of TuRo (see 1990)
Grand Prize Futurity Winner	Crossroad's Movin On Up Breeders: Dorothy Hart and Ruth Appleby Owners: Tony and Sherri Christian

52nd Annual Specialty Show, May 8–12, Frederick, MD

BOB	Ch. Kimber-D Pinebrook Dusty Road Breeder: Travis Harris Owners: Travis Harris, Arlene Perret and Dale Harris
BOS	Carlon's Red Hot Breeders: Eileen McClintock, Bob Long and Lucky and Donna Watson Owners: Bob and Tom Long
Grand Prize Futurity Winner	Virgo's Celebration Breeder/Owners: Owen G., Jr., and Gina Proctor
HIT	Karosel's Krystal Klear Breeder/Owner: Ella M. DuPree

53rd Annual Specialty Show, April 27 to May 1, 1996, Frederick, MD

BOB   Ch. TuRo's Futurian of Cachet
Breeders: Clay Haviland, Sandy Roberts and Elizabeth Esacove
Owners: Jeff and Nan-Eisley Bennett

BOS   Ch. Kiebla's Tradition of TuRo (see 1991)

Grand Prize Futurity Winner   C-Era Dar's DejaVu
Breeder/Owners: Carolyn Pressley, John Keil and
Darlene Spyra

HIT   Bylin's Traveling Whirlwind, CDX
Breeder/Owners: Linda Liguori and Lorraine Capurso

54th Annual Specialty Show, May 5–9, 1997, Frederick, MD

BOB   Ch. Hi-Tech Johnny J of Boxerton
Breeder: Alison and Jefferson Crowther
Owners: Dr. William and Zoila Truesdale

BOS   Ch. Kiebla's Tradition of TuRo (see 1990)

Grand Prize Futurity Winner   Mistyvalley Vancroft Bo Derek
Breeder/Owners: Brenda Grice, Deborah Clark and
Marcia Adams

HIT   Ch. Sunchase's Hollywood Hype
Breeder/Owner: Tracy L. Hendrickson

55th Annual Specialty Show, May 3–8, 1998, Frederick, MD

BOB   Ch. Hi-Tech Johnny J of Boxerton (see 1997)

BOS   Ch. Huffand's Obladah of Arriba
Breeders: Linda Huffman, Carole Connolly and Dr. Ted Fickes
Owners: Philip Koenig and Barbara Gibson

Grand Prize Futurity Winner   Zephyr's He Said, She Said
Breeder: Sharon Simpson
Owners: Priscilla and James Kilman and Sharon Simpson

HIT   BJ's Royal Glow Topaz Gold
                             Breeders: Tammy and Robert Amen
                             Owner: Brenda Durbin

56th Annual Specialty Show, May 10–14, 1999, Frederick, MD

BOB   Ch. Vancroft's Primetime
                             Breeder: Deborah Clark, Marcia Adams and Jimmy Stevens
                             Owners: Deborah Clark and Marcia Adams

BOS   Ch. Holly Lane's Créme de Menthe
                             Breeder: Eileen McClintock
                             Owners: Deborah Clark and Marcia Adams

Grand Prize Futurity Winner Rummer Run's Major General
                             Breeder/Owner: Steve and Ann Anderson

HIT   Ch. Sunchase's Zero to Hero
                             Breeder/Owner: Tracy L. Hendrickson

High in Agility Trial   Karosel's Brass Ring, NA
                             Breeder/Owner: Ella M. Dupree

Top Twenty Winners, 1989–99

1989

Ch. Rochil's Grand Marshall, SOM, Fawn Dog,
wh. 2/16/85, d. 11/1996
Sire: Ch. Har-Vel's Gold Express
Dam: Ch. Rochil's Kalista of Marburl
Breeders/Owners: Perry and Sandi Combest

"Maxx," an ABC Sire of Merit, won twenty-one
all-breed Best in Shows and ninety-four Group
firsts, as well as nineteen Specialties including the
1986 ABC Regional. He was Group 2 at
Westminster in 1989. Sire of twenty-five
champions. Handled by Michael Shepherd.

1990

Ch. Merrilane's Knockout, SOM, wh. 4/85,
d. 4/92
Sire: Ch. Merrilane's April Holiday, SOM
Dam: Ch. Jacquet's Mercer
Breeder/Owner: Eleanor Linderholm Wood

"KO" sired eighteen champions and won three
Groups and ten Specialties, always handled by
breeder/owner Eleanor Linderholm Wood. He is
an ABC Sire of Merit.

1991

Ch. Kiebla's Tradition of TuRo, DOM, wh. 1/20/88
Sire—TuRo's Escapade
Dam—Ch. Kiebla's Mercy
Breeder: Kitti Barker
Owners: Bruce and Jeanne Korson, Kitti Barker, Sandy Roberts and Liz Esacove

"Tiggin" was Best of Breed at ABC in 1991, 1992 and 1993. She was BOS at ABC in 1994, 1996 and 1997, as well as Best Veteran in Show at ABC 1999. She was BOB at the ABC Regional in 1990, 1991 and 1992. Tiggin is an ABC Dam of Merit with four champions from her only litter whelped a few days before her 7th birthday. She was Group 1 at Westminster in 1993 and won fifty all-breed Best in Shows.

1992

Ch. Hi-Tech Arbitrage, LOM, wh. 5/8/90
Sire: Ch. Fiero's Tally-Ho Tailo, LOM
Dam: Ch. Boxerton Hollyhock, DOM
Breeder: JoAnne Sheffler
Owners: Dr. and Mrs. William Truesdale

"Biff," an ABC Legion of Merit Sire, won forty-nine Best in Shows, twenty-seven Specialties and 140 Group Firsts. He was Westminster Working Group winner in 1994, as well as ABC Best of Breed winner in the same year.

1993

Ch. Moon Valley's Main Attraction SOM, wh. 5/10/91
Sire: Ch. Tall Oaks Desert Dazzler
Dam: Ch. Moon Valley's Image
Breeder: Ida Baum
Owners: Ray Culberson and Bill Weber

"Main Attraction" is a multiple Group and Best in Show winner. He is an ABC Sire of Merit.

1994

Ch. Vancroft's Primetime, SOM, wh. 6/7/91, d. 8/30/99
Sire: Ch. Misty Valley's Curtain Call, SOM
Dam: Ch. Vancroft's Vogue
Breeders: Deborah Clark, Marcia Adams and Jimmy Sawyer
Owners: Deborah Clark and Marcia Adams

"O.D." is an ABC Sire of Merit. He was BOB at Westminster in 1997 and at ABC in 1999, at almost 8 years old. During his career, he won five Best in Shows, forty-one Group Firsts and twelve Specialty Best in Shows.

1995

Ch. Cayman's Black Bart, SOM, wh. 6/11/91
Sire: Ch. Vandown-King's Fire Alert
Dam: Ch. Cayman's Sweet Nandi
Breeder: Sydney Brown
Owners: Michael and Monique O'Connor and
Manuel Casado

"Bart" is an ABC Sire of Merit, a Group winner,
and an Award of Merit winner at ABC 1994
and 1995.

1996

Ch. Sirrocco's Kiss By the Book, wh. 10/9/94,
d. 7/25/99
Sire: Ch. Golden Haze Tuxedo, LOM
Dam: Sirrocco's Kiss and Tell
Breeders: Diane Mallett and Kathleen Gould
Owner: Diane Mallett

"Jillian" won seventeen Group firsts and two Best
in Shows. She was #1 Boxer in 1997.

1997

Ch. Rummer Run's Stardust, wh. 6/9/95
Sire: Ch. Hi-Tech Arbitrage, LOM
Dam: Ch. Rummer Run's Tattle Tail
Breeders/Owners: Steven G. and Ann B. Anderson

To date, "Stardust" has won twenty-five Best in
Shows and eighty-one Group Firsts. She is a 1998
and 1999 ABC Award of Merit winner.

1998

Ch. Huffand's Obladah of Arriba, wh. 1/2/95
Sire: Ch. Ewo's Tiebreaker
Dam: Ch. Huffand's Obsession of Arriba
Breeders: Linda Huffman, Carole Connolly and
Dr. Ted Fickes
Owners: Phillip Koenig and Barbara Gibson

"Tony" was BOS at ABC in 1998, and an Award of
Merit winner in 1999.

1999

Ch. Storybook Rip It Up, wh. 10/1/96
Sire: Ch. Cherkei's Ultimate High
Dam: Ch. Storybook's Make Believe
Breeders: Skip and Linda Abel
Owners: Cheryl and Keith Robbins

"Jake" is a multiple Best in Show winner and an
Award of Merit winner at ABC 1999. He is being
actively campaigned as of this writing, with multiple
Group and Best in Show wins to date.

ADDITIONAL ABC BEST OF BREED WINNERS

While some of the Top Twenty winners have also won Best of Breed at the American Boxer Club National Specialty, and are so noted previously, that is not always the case. Here follows information on the additional dogs who have won this coveted award since 1989.

1989

Ch. Berena's Tribute to Fa-Fa, SOM, wh. 1/9/87, d. 3/19/97
Sire: Ch. Wagner's Wilvirday Famous Amos, SOM
Dam: Summerbird Leading Lady, DOM
Breeder: Bernard R. and Rena J. Toon
Owners: Larry and Gene Neumann and Bernie and Rena Toon

"Britt," a Sire of Merit, also took the ABC Regional BOB in 1988. He won four Best in Shows, more than twenty-five Group Firsts and thirteen Best in Specialty shows. He was Best of Breed at Westminster in 1990.

1990

Ch. Heldenbrand's Jet Breaker, SOM, wh. 4/19/88, d. 4/1/98
Sire: Ch. Heldenbrand's Heart Breaker, SOM
Dam: Heldenbrand's Jetta Jovina, DOM
Breeder: E. Heldenbrand
Owners: Jeff Bennett and Judy Hunt

"Jet Breaker" was also BOB at the ABC Regional in 1989. He is an ABC Sire of Merit and the winner of eighty Group Firsts and twenty all-breed Best in Shows.

1995

Ch. Kimber-D Pinebrook Dusty Road, wh. 4/20/94
Sire: Ch. Pinebrook's Innuendo, SOM
Dam: Pinebrook's Shades of Autumn
Breeder: Travis Harris
Owners: Travis Harris, Dale Harris and Arlene Perret

"Dusty" won two Group Firsts, amateur owner-handled.

1996

Ch. TuRo's Futurian of Cachet, wh. 10/19/92, d. 12/10/96
Sire: Ch. Cachet's High River Gambler
Dam: TuRo's Charisma of Garnsey
Breeders: C. G. Haviland, Sandy Roberts and Elizabeth Esacove
Owners: Jeff Bennett and Nan Eisley-Bennett

"Future" was also BOB at the ABC Regional in 1995. He took Group 1 at Westminster in 1996. He was Best Puppy in the 1993 ABC Futurity, #1 Boxer for 1996 and winner of over 100 Group Firsts and twenty-six Best in Shows.

1997 and 1998

Ch. Hi-Tech Johnny J of Boxerton, wh. 6/2/95
Sire: Ch. Hi-Tech's Aristocrat, SOM
Dam: Ch. Boxerton Crown Imperial, DOM
Breeders: Alison and Jefferson Crowther.

Owners: Dr. William Truesdale and
Zoila Truesdale.

"Johnny" was also BOB at the ABC Regional in
1996. As of September 1999, he was #1 Boxer and
ranked #3 among all breeds. He has won 134
Group Firsts and thirty Best in Shows to date.

OBEDIENCE STARS

High in Trial winners at the American Boxer Club National since 1995 are as follows.

1995

Ch. U-CD Karosel's Krystal Clear, CDX, OA, AD,
OAC, OGC, OJC, CGC, TD1, wh. 2/5/92,
d. 9/14/99
Sire: Ch. Harlyn Top Priority
Dam: Ch. Foxwoods Krystal Karosel, DOM, CDX
Breeder/Owner: Ella M. Dupree

"Ida" finished her championship in only six weeks
at age 4, after producing two litters. Her ABC HIT
score, from Novice B, was 197.

1996

Bylin's Traveling Whirlwind, CDX, wh. 1/29/92
Sire: Ch. Huffand's Sarazan Traveller
Dam: Bylin's Life's a Breeze, CD
Breeders/Owners: Linda Liguori and Lorraine
Capurso

"Whirlwind" achieved a score of 195 from
Novice B.

1997

Ch. Sunchase's Hollywood Hype, CD,
wh. 5/12/91
Sire: Ch. Rochil's Grande Marshall
Dam: Ch. Sunchase's Solar Eclipse
Breeder/Owner/Handler: Tracy L. Hendrickson

"Kimmie" achieved a score of 195½ from Novice
B at the ABC trial. She is the dam of Ch.
Sunchase's Suicide Blonde, CDX, NAJ, NA.

1998

BJ's Royal Glow Topaz Gold, wh. 4/22/94
Sire: Amen's Sundance Kid
Dam: Princess Arabella Amen
Breeders: Tammy and Robert Amen
Owner/Handler: Brenda Durbin

When she entered the show, owner Brenda Durbin
was unaware that ABC was the breed National!
"Topaz Gold" took top honors with a score of
196½ from Novice B.

1999

Ch. Sunchase's Zero to Hero, wh. 11/22/97
Sire: Ch. Holly Lane's Spin a Dream
Dam: Ch. Sunchase's Fashionably Late, CDX
Breeder/Owner: Tracy L. Hendrickson

"Spencer" was the 1998 ABC Regional Winners Dog. He won his 1999 ABC HIT in a run-off, with a score of 196+ from Novice B.

A "SINGULAR ACHIEVEMENT!"

To date, the only Boxer to achieve the title of OTCh—AKC Obedience Trial Champion—is:

OTCh Marilyn's Tinamarie of Bropat, UDX, TD, wh. 1/20/87, d. 6/96
Sire: Ch. Bropat's Red Alert of Asgard, SOM
Dam: Rumac's Everything Nice
Breeders: John and Ruth McFarland
Owners: Marilyn and Steve Krejci

"Tina" achieved her OTCh title in June 1991 under judge Pat Scully, the late Marilyn Krejci handling. She was also the first Boxer to win the coveted UDX title. In the course of her brilliant career, she won many High In Trial and High Combined awards against some of the sport's best and brightest. To date, Tina is still the only Boxer to win the OTCh.

The second Boxer to achieve the UDX is My Sweet Suzette, UDX, AX, AXJ. Bred and owned by James and Ruth Hutchins and handled by Jim, Suzette won the High Combined honors at ABC in 1997.

OTCh Marilyn's Tinamarie of Bropat is, to date, the only Boxer OTCh title holder. She is shown here with her beloved owner/handler, the late Marilyn Krecji. (Meyer Photo)

SCHUTZHUND CELEBRITIES

The United States Boxer Association presented awards to the following dogs in 1998 during the Working Champion of the Year Competition.

USBA Working Champion of the Year

Ivo vom Hafen, BH, SchH3, IPO3, ZTP, wh. 9/5/95
Sire: Agassi v. Ellinghaus, SchH1, IPO1, AD
Dam: Eyleen vom Hafen, BH, SchH3, ZTP
Breeder: Udo and Ilone Schweers (Germany)
Owners: George and Cathy Markos

Ivo repeated his 1998 Working Champion achievement in 1999.

USBA High Scoring Tracking and High Scoring Obedience Dog

Xenia von Sparta, BH, SchH1, IPO2, CDX, TR1, Cert. Police Tracking Dog, TDI registered Therapy Dog, wh. 11/27/93
Sire: ATIBOX, VDH, Ch. John v. Maximilian, SchH1, AD
Dam: Ve v. Sparta, SchH2, AD
Breeder: Toni Piasentin (Germany)
Owners: Cathy and George Markos

"Xenia" is the first and only IPO-titled female Boxer in the United States. She is also the first to earn a Level 2 title in Schutzhund.

Ch. Flintwood's Linebacker. (Fleischman)

Important Kennels

This list is representative of the many Boxer breeders over the years who have contributed so much to the breed. It is not an exclusive list, but one intended to illustrate that the Boxer is, and has been, in creative and dedicated hands throughout the years.

ARRIBA BOXERS

Begun in 1964, the Arriba Boxers were in close geographical proximity to both Salgray and Flintwood kennels, and to these breeders Dr. Theodore Fickes credits much of his early success. His "plain" foundation bitch, Nahum's Arriba, was a Ch. Eu-Bet's Typecutter daughter who produced Ch. Arriba's Amulet by Ch. Mazelaine's Early Times. Amulet, in turn, bred to Ch. Capriana's Renegade, produced the three champion sisters Carioca, Calypso and Castanet. From these beginnings, a string of Arriba champions continues to this day. Notables include Ch. Arriba's Knight Revue, SOM (fifteen champions), who was WD and BW at the ABC Specialty in 1972; and the unforgettable Ch. Arriba's Prima Donna. "Suzie" won twenty-three all-breed Best in Shows and took top honors at Westminster in 1970, the only Boxer bitch ever to do so. There have been to date six Arriba ABC Sires of Merit and four ABC Dams of Merit. The most recent SOM is one of the top Boxers of 1997–98, Ch. Arriba Talisman Ego, co-bred with Virginia Shames. "Briar" achieved this honor just as he turned 4 years of age, one of the youngest Sires of Merit in breed history.

Ch. Cherkei's Ultimate High with handler Michael Shepherd. (G. Glazbrook)

CHERKEI BOXERS

Cheryl and Keith Robbins of Georgia bred their first litter in 1977 and since that time have owned or bred fifty-seven champions. They are especially proud of five Best in Show winners: Ch. Cherkei's Son-of-a-Gun (a Ch. Salgray's Good Grief son), Ch. Arriba's Cherkei Oh-Boy, Ch. Cherkei's High Cotton, Ch. Arriba Talisman Ego and Ch.

Storybook Rip It Up, a son of Ch. Cherkei's Ultimate High and the winner of the ABC Top Twenty in 1999. Cheryl handled many of her own dogs to their titles, was a very successful professional handler and is now a sought-after judge of the breed. She was proud to judge Dogs at ABC in 1998. Keith continues to judge Sweepstakes and intends to apply for his judge's license in the near future.

THE FLINTWOOD BOXERS

Dr. and Mrs. Lloyd Flint of Massachusetts established their Flintwood Boxers in the mid-1950s with the purchase of two litter sisters, the soon-to-be champions Sans Souci and Morganshern of Kresthallo. They were both Bang Away granddaughters. The Flints took a very scientific approach to dog breeding: Both sisters were bred to Bang Away's top-producing son, Ch. Barrage of Quality Hill, LOM. Their progeny, in turn, was bred back to aunt, uncle or cousin. This relatively close (or line) breeding established a definite Flintwood type. Flintwood dogs were known for especially beautiful heads and toplines, as well as overall excellence.

From 1956–65, in only seventeen breedings, twenty-six champions were born. They included four American Boxer Club Sires of Merit and two Dams of Merit, plus the two foundation bitches. Ch. Arriba's Prima Donna, the Westminster winner in 1970, was sired by Ch. Flintwood's Live Ammo. Ch. Hi-Tech Arbitrage, SOM, winner of the Westminster Working Group in 1994, traces back to

Flintwood through his sire, Ch. Fiero's Tally-Ho Tailo, LOM. Prima Donna was owned by Dr. Theodore Fickes and co-owned by Dr. and Mrs. P. J. Pagano. Dr. Fickes' Arriba Kennels in Massachusetts, and now in Virginia, have contributed many foundation bitches to other people's breeding programs—notably those of Woods End, Huffand, New Dawn and Karjean. Those bitches were a product, in part, of breeding to Flintwood lines.

HI-TECH BOXERS

Dr William and Zoila ("Tina") Truesdale of Massachusetts are currently the breeders/owners of nearly sixty champions and four generations of Best in Show winners. Established as "Hi-Tech" in 1984, they are owners of Ch. Hi-Tech Arbitrage, LOM, a Westminster Group winner in 1994. They are co-breeders of the current #3 all-breeds, Ch. Hi-Tech Johnny J of Boxerton, twice a winner of BOB at the ABC National Specialty in 1997 and 1998. The breeding of Hi-Tech bitches to the great show dog and producer leased from breeder Ingrid Feder by the Truesdales, Ch. Fiero's Tally-Ho Tailo, LOM, has resulted in many of Hi-Tech's winners and producers, including Arbitrage and Ch. Hi-Tech Current Event, SOM. Bill presided over the Futurity at ABC in 1999 and currently serves on the ABC Board of Directors.

HOLLY LANE

The Holly Lane kennels of Dr. E. A. and Eileen McClintock of Kansas were founded in the early 1960s. Ch. Holly Lane's Windstorm, Legion of Merit, is the all-time top-producing bitch in breed history, with eleven champions to her credit. Windstorm was a daughter of Ch. Brayshaw's Masquerader out of Ch. Holly Lane's Cookie, the first Holly Lane champion and herself a daughter of the Flint's Ch. Flintwood's Sundowner. Although Dr. McClintock passed away in 1980, Eileen is still actively breeding and showing today, and Holly Lane has given the fancy five ABC Sires of Merit and four ABC Dams of Merit to date. Ch. Holly Lane's Spin A Dream, a brindle dog owned by Mr. and Mrs. J. L. Streicher, is a multiple all-breed Best in Show winner whelped in 1995 and campaigned through 1998. The fawn bitch Ch. Carlon's Red Hot, co-bred by Eileen McClintock, Bob Long and Lucky and Donna Watson, was the American Boxer Club WB and BW and BOS in 1995. In 1999, Ch. Holly Lane's Crème de Menthe was BOS at ABC over fifty bitch specials.

JACQUET KENNELS

Richard Tomita and William Scolnik began their New Jersey Jacquet line when they bred the future Ch. Jacquet's Ronel Micah in 1971. Since that date, Jacquet has finished the championships of more than 170 AKC champions and more than 250 worldwide. At present, there are five Jacquet Sires of Merit and six Jacquet Dams of Merit. Jacquet has consistently won the ABC awards for Kennel Breeding the Most Champions and Kennel Finishing the Most Champions. Ch. Happy Ours Fortune of Jacquet, SOM, sired over fifty-five

Ch. Jacquet's Ruddyard. (P. Phillips)

worked for two summers as a young woman at the famous Mazelaine Kennels of Jack and Mazie Wagner. Her foundation bitch, Merrilane's Mad Passion, CD, LOM, is the second top-producing bitch of all time, with ten champion offspring. Ch. Merrilane's April Fashion, LOM, owned by Coleman Cook, sired twenty-three champions and was very influential in leaving behind progeny who became important as the foundation of other important breeding programs. One of Eleanor's greatest personal thrills was winning the ABC Top Twenty competition in 1990 with Ch. Merrilane's Knockout, SOM, owner-handled and co-owner-bred along with Jacquet Kennels.

THE SALGRAY KENNELS

The Salgray kennels of Phyllis and Daniel Hamilburg of Brookline, Massachusetts, gave the Boxer new elegance and style, and they must be considered important architects in creating this "new" Boxer.

The first Salgray champion was finished in 1955: Ch. Sally of Grayarlin. Sally was purchased from Jane Kamp (now the well-known handler and judge, Jane Forsyth) and her Grayarlin Kennels in 1952. In 1954, the Hamilburgs purchased a bitch who was to become Ch. Slipper of Grayarlin. When they bred her to the Bang Away son, Ch. Barrage of Quality Hill, LOM (sire of forty-five champions), they produced Ch. Salgray's Battle Chief. He eventually sired twenty-three champions,

champions worldwide and is one of the most influential of the Jacquet Boxers. Ch. Jacquet's Cambridge Fortune was the top Boxer bitch of 1994 and a multiple Best in Show winner, while Ch. Jacquet's Noire is one of the stars of 1999. Jacquet looks forward to campaigning Ch. Jacquet's Ruddyard in the year 2000.

MERRILANE BOXERS

Eleanor Linderholm Wood and her Merrilane Boxers of California, and now of Arizona, have accounted for seventy-seven champions since 1971. In love with the Boxer from an early age, "Ellie" among them the famous "F" litter of six champions whelped in 1961.

More important than the distinction of six champions in one litter, however, was that the litter included two dogs and a bitch who would have a great influence on the breed through their offspring. They were Ch. Salgray's Fashion Plate, SOM (sixty-three champions), Ch. Salgray's Flying High, LOM (twenty-seven champions) and the bitch Ch. Salgray's Flaming Ember, who in turn produced Ch. Salgray's Ambush, LOM (thirty-three champions).

Salgray Boxers and their famous descendents changed the way many looked at the breed then and now. They were, in general, taller, more refined and more elegant than the breed had been in its infancy in America. The Hamilburg's daughter, Jane Guy, continues to breed the Salgray line into the millennium.

SCARBOROUGH BOXERS

The Scarborough Boxers of Jason and Virginia Zurflieh of Florida were established in 1973 with the purchase of the Shadrack daughter, Ch. Scher-

Ch. Merrilane's April Fashion, LOM, sire of 23 champions.

Khoun's Tarantella. When bred to Ch. Gray Roy's Minstrel Boy, "Tara" gave the breed the ABC Sire of Merit Ch. Scarborough Silversmith and the ABC Dam of Merit Scarborough Soliloquy. Ch. Trefoil's Scarborough Fair was Group winner and WB, BW at the ABC Regional in 1976. Scarborough's second SOM was Ch. Scarborough Norman Knight (by Ch. Huffand's Nice Enough, SOM). Ch. Scarborough Living Proof (by Ch. Golden Haze Tuxedo, LOM) attained DOM status in 1998.

SIRRAH CREST

Dr. and Mrs. R. C. Harris founded their Sirrah (Harris spelled backwards) Crest Kennels of California in the late 1930s with the purchase of a puppy who grew up to be Ch. Marshall v. Bismark. Unfortunately, Marshall was not from sterling bloodlines, so the Harris's were referred to John and Mazie Wagner for advice on what to do next. They spent considerable time at Mazelaine and departed with a Dorian son, Duke Cronian, and an Utz daughter, Quida of Mazelaine. In 1941, they saw Dorian's superlative daughter, Ch. Nocturne of

Ch. Bang Away of Sirrah Crest, the top-winning and top-producing Boxer of all time.

including seven champion stud dogs, at the kennels. Their program was an intensely linebred one (as in granddaughter to grandsire, nephew to aunt), and in Bang Away's five-generation pedigree (space for sixty-two names), there are only thirty individual dogs. Always careful not to double-up on known faults, and by staying within the crosses going back to Utz and Dorian, the Harris's established their own type: beautiful toplines, excellent angulation and correct shoulders. After Bang Away was born, the dissolution of the kennel meant that the Harris's never got to see what they would have thought ideal—A Bang Away or Break Away (his litter brother) daughter bred to the uncle. However, witnessing Bang Away's amazing prepotency was reward enough.

TREFOIL BOXERS

The Trefoil Boxers of Connecticut's David and Stephanie Abraham began in 1970 with the purchase of the future Legion of Merit Sire, Am. and Can. Ch. Gray Roy's Minstrel Boy, sire of twenty-four champions. Since that time, always breeding on a small scale, the Abrahams have owned or bred over thirty champions. These include the ABC Sires of Merit Ch. Trefoil's Choir Boy and Ch. Trefoil's Dylan of Donessle, and the ABC Dams of Merit Kaseba's Showgirl and Trefoil's Flashpoint. David and Stephanie are both active in ABC activities—David serving on the Standard Committee and Stephanie as a member of the ABC Board of Directors and Chairman of Publicity and Judges' Education. Both are AKC judges, and Stephanie presided over Bitches and

Mazelaine, and bought her daughter, Kantatrix, on the spot. While she did not have her mother's great conformation and especially dynamic showmanship, the bloodlines were enough to convince the Harris's that they needed her in their breeding program. Using Kantatrix wisely, along with her brother and a nephew, meant that by the time Bang Away came along eight years later, he had in his lineage crosses to Nocturne no less than six times. Mrs. Harris attributes Bang Away's legendary showmanship to Nocturne's genes.

Sirrah Crest bred Boxers for only nine years. In that time, they gave us twenty-nine champions and two Best in Show winners—in about four generations. At one time, they had about sixty Boxers,

Ch. Gray Roy's Minstrel Boy, LOM, the sire of twenty-four champions for Trefoil Boxers. (J. Ashbey)

Intersex at the 1995 ABC, while David did the same honors in 1999.

TuRo Boxers

Sandy Roberts and Elizabeth Esacove of Texas have been actively breeding and exhibiting under the TuRo name since the 1970s. However, Liz's associations with Boxers go back much further, and she campaigned Ch. Ringmaster's Olympian, whelped in 1968, under the Esa Lyn banner. Ch. TuRo's Whisper of 5Ts, DOM (a daughter of Ch. Benjoman of 5Ts, LOM [sire of thirty-eight champions]), owned by Dr. Robert Burke (Marquam

Hills), produced Ch. Marquam Hill's Traper of 5Ts, LOM, who, with sixty-seven champions, is the second top-producing stud dog in the United States.

Among their many champions, TuRo has bred or co-bred a remarkable three Westminster Group winners: Ch. TuRo's Cachet, Ch. TuRo's Futurian of Cachet and Ch. Kiebla's Tradition of TuRo, DOM ("Tiggin"). Tiggin is the top winning bitch in breed history with fifty Best in Shows.

Vancroft Boxers

Deborah Clark and Marcia Adams of Florida have had considerable success in a relatively short time. Their foundation bitch, purchased in 1985, was Ch. Gerhard's String of Pearls. A Ch. Scarborough Norman Knight, SOM, daughter, she became an ABC Dam of Merit. In only fifteen years, Vancroft has bred and/or finished almost forty champions, including Ch. Misty Valley Vancroft Bo Derek, Grand Prize Futurity winner at ABC 1997; Ch. Holly Lane's Crème de Menthe, BOS at ABC 1999; and Ch. Vancroft's Primetime, SOM, Top Twenty winner in 1994, a five-time Best in Show winner and Best of Breed at ABC 1999 at almost 8 years of age.

Woods End

The Woods End Kennels was established in Connecticut by Pat and Jack Billhardt in the early

Ch. Trefoil's Lili Marlene. (S. Abraham)

BEST IN
SHOW
ATUR ALABAMA
KENNEL CLUB
FALL 1994
PHOTO BY
PATTY SOSA

Ch. Vancroft's Primetime. (M. Adams)

1970s with the purchase of the foundation bitch, Ch. Arriba's Dresden Souvenir (Ch. Gray Roy's Minstrel Boy x Arriba's Gin 'n Tonic). Since that time, Woods End is proud to have bred and owned twenty-three champions. Among these are the notable Ch. Woods End Crown Sable, SOM, a multiple Group winner and sire to date of twenty-eight champions, and his younger brother, Ch. Woods End Million Heir, SOM, winner of nine Best in Shows. Ch. Woods End Chasin' Rainbows,

Ch. Woods End Crown Sable. (Visual Concepts Photography)

a full sister to Crown Sable, produced Ch. Hi-Tech Aristocrat, SOM, when bred to Ch. Hi-Tech Arbitrage.

(Marcia Adams)

Bibliography

Abraham, Stephanie. "Matchmaking." *American Kennel Club Gazette* (August, 1994).

American Boxer Charitable Foundation, Inc., "A History of the American Boxer Club," "Top Twenty."

American Boxer Club. *Boxer Club News*. Morris Plains, NJ: American Boxer Club. Marie Thorne, Ed. 1945; Carl and Alice Wood, Eds. 1950 and 1951 (March 1945, May 1945, July 1945, September 1945, March 1950, Spring 1951).

American Kennel Club, http://www.akc.org. "Companion Animal Recovery," "American Kennel Club Good Citizen," "AKC Regulations for Agility Trials," "AKC Obedience Department," "AKC Regulations for Junior Showmanship."

American Temperament Test Society, www.atts.org. "Description of the Temperament Test."

Baldwin, Charles H., DVM. "Lyme Disease in the Cat." *Cats Magazine* (July 1991): 22– 23.

Blue Seal Feeds. "Consumer Information Chart." Londonderry, NH: March 1994.

Burkholder, Craton, MD, *Emergency Care for Dogs and Cats*. New York, NY: Michael Kesend Publishing, 1987.

Cairns, Julie. *The Golden Retriever*. New York, NY: Howell Book House, 1999.

Campbell, Suzie, Ed. *American Boxer Club Anniversary Album*. American Boxer Club, 1985.

Canine Companions for Independence, www.caninecompanions.org. "Frequently Asked Questions." *Delta Society Overview*, http://petsforum.com/deltasociety.

Eukanuba, www.eukanuba.com. "Senior Citizens."

FCI, www.fci.be/english/info. "General Information."

Fraser, Clarence M., Ed. *Merck Veterinary Manual*. Rahway, NJ: Merck and Co., 1991.

Keene, Bruce W., DVM. "Heart Muscle Disease in Dogs." *The Boxer Review* (November 1988): 10–11.

Lust, George. ("Hip Dysplasia in Dogs." *The Boxer Review* (November 1988): 14–16.

Meyer, Lorraine C. *Your Boxer*. Fairfax, VA: Denlinger's, 1973.

Miller, Harry. *Common Sense Book of Puppy and Dog Care*. New York, NY: Bantam Books, 1987.

Moulton, Jack E., Ed. *Tumors in Domestic Animals* (3rd ed.). Berkeley and Los Angeles, California: University of California Press, 1990.

Rosenthal, Alice, Ed. *Dog News*. Cincinnati, Ohio: February 1964, July 1965, July 1969.

Stockmann, Friederun. *My Life With Boxers*. Translated by Cal Gruver. Sauk Rapids, MN: Classic Pet Books, 1968.

Tomita, Richard. *The World of the Boxer*. Neptune City, NJ: T.F.H. Publications, 1998.

United States Boxer Association, http://members.aol.com/Usabox. Home Page and Linked Articles.

Vasey, Diane, Ed. "Emergency First Aid." *American Kennel Club Gazette* (February 1995): 46–51.

Wagner, John P. *The Boxer*. New York, NY: Orange Judd Publishing Co., 1953.

———. "Lecture to Professional Judges Forum," NY, 1945. As reprinted in *Dog News*, Alice Rosenthal, ed., (February, 1957): 16 and 28.

Welborn Pet Hospital, www.welbornpet.com. "Keep Your Pet Healthy in the Later Years." Bernie Robe, DVM.

Index